Mother At Our Side
Mary's Role in the Spiritual Life

by
Edward Carter, S.J.

Mother At Our Side

Mary's Role in the Spiritual Life

by
Edward Carter, S.J.

Edited & Published by,
Faith Publishing Co.
P.O. Box 237
Milford, OH 45150

The Publisher recognizes and accepts that the final authority regarding any apparitions and/or supernatural messages as referred to in this book rests with the Holy See of Rome, to whose judgment we willingly submit.

—The Publisher

IMPRIMI POTEST: Bradley M. Schaeffer, SJ

NIHIL OBSTAT: Edward B. Brueggeman, SJ

IMPRIMATUR: Rev. R. Daniel Conlon
Chancellor and Vicar General
Archdiocese of Cincinnati

June, 1993

Published by Faith Publishing Company
For additional copies, write to:

Faith Publishing Company
P.O. Box 237
Milford, Ohio 45150
or
The Riehle Foundation
P.O. Box 7
Milford, Ohio 45150

Library of Congress Catalog No.: 93-072114

ISBN: 1-880033-07-0

Table of Contents

Acknowledgments

The author acknowledges the use of excerpts from the following material:

Scripture texts used in this work are taken from *The New American Bible with Revised New Testament* Copyright © 1986 by the Confraternity of Christian Doctrine, 3211 4th Street, N.E., Washington, D.C. 20017-1194 and are used by permission of copyright owner. All rights reserved.

To the Priests, Our Lady's Beloved Sons, The Marian Movement of Priests, St. Francis, Maine.

Live the Messages, by D.R. Golob, Harahan, Louisiana.

Our Lady's Peace Plan from Heaven, TAN Books and Publishers, Inc., Rockford, Illinois.

The Fatima Crusader, Summer, 1992, Constable, New York.

I Am Your Jesus of Mercy, 3 volumes, Riehle Foundation, Milford, Ohio.

To Mary The Immaculate Heart
Who Leads Us To The Heart Of Jesus

E.C.

Preface

It was the hour of Jesus' agony. He hung on a cross, on a hill called Calvary. He had already suffered excruciating pain. He had been brutally scourged—can we comprehend what this did to Jesus? He had been crowned with thorns. He had carried the heavy cross and then was mercilessly nailed to it. After all this, the excruciating suffering continued as the weight of His body pulled downward against the nail-inflicted wounds of His hands and feet. Besides the intense physical suffering, there was the spiritual anguish which pierced Jesus' Heart.

Amidst this unfathomable suffering, Jesus spoke to Mary and John as they stood at the foot of the cross: *Woman, behold, your son.* Then He said to the disciple, *Behold, your mother.* (*Jn.* 19: 26-7).

John represented all of us. In giving Mary to him as spiritual mother, Jesus was also giving Mary to all of us as our spiritual mother.

In these our times, the spiritual motherhood of Mary is being manifested in an extraordinary fashion. There have been alleged apparitions of Mary in many parts of the world. Many seem to bear the marks of authenticity. A small number of these apparition sites have already received official Church approval. Regarding the others, we await the Church's final judgment and express our willingness to submit to her ultimate decision.

Why such an extraordinary proliferation of Marian apparitions and messages? Because we live in extraordinary times. Mary is telling us that the Church and the world are experiencing a time of great crisis brought about by an unprecedented wave of sin which has been sweeping across the face of the earth.

Through Mary, God is using extraordinary means to call us to conversion. Mary tells us that her Immaculate Heart is leading the Church and the world along the way of conversion as she leads us in an extraordinary fashion to Jesus, the Light of the world. She is beseeching us in a special way to give our assistance to help fulfill the mission God has entrusted to her.

In writing this book on Mary's role in the Christian life, I have drawn upon the teaching of Scripture and upon Church documents. I have used messages Mary has given at apparition sites, as well as the locutions or messages allegedly given to certain of her chosen ones over and above those associated with her apparitions. I have also used the thoughts of other theologians. Minor portions of this book have been drawn from some of my previously published books.

Using all of the above sources—and others not listed—I have tried to delineate Mary's role as spiritual Mother to us. In doing so, I have also tried to give an overview of the spiritual life. My prayerful hope is that the book will help the reader grow in appreciation of Mary's motherhood regarding us. Indeed, we go to the Father through Christ in the Holy Spirit, with Mary as Mother at our side.

Edward Carter, S.J.
Xavier University

one

Mother Of Christ

Then the angel said to her, "Do not be afraid, Mary, for you have found favor with God. Behold, you will conceive in your womb and bear a son, and you shall name him Jesus."
...But Mary said to the angel, "How can this be, since I have no relations with a man?" And the angel said to her in reply, "The Holy Spirit will come upon you, and the power of the Most High will overshadow you. Therefore the child to be born will be called holy, the Son of God. ..." Mary said, "Behold, I am the handmaid of the Lord. May it be done to me according to your word." (Lk. 1:30-38).

"The Blessed Virgin was eternally predestined, in conjuction with the Incarnation of the Divine Word, to be the Mother of God. By decree of divine Providence, she served on earth as the loving mother of the divine Redeemer, an associate of unique nobility, and the Lord's humble handmaid. She conceived, brought forth, and nourished Christ. She presented Him to the Father in the temple, and was united with Him in suffering as He died on the cross. In an utterly singular way she cooperated by her obedience, faith, hope, and burning charity in the Savior's work of restoring supernatural life to souls." (*Vatican* II).[1]

The above words of Scripture and of the Second Vatican Council tell us of a most awesome truth—that Mary truly is the Mother of Jesus, that she truly is the Mother of God.

To speak of Mary, then, is to speak of Christ. Mary's entire life was centered on Christ. No human has ever followed Christ as closely as has Mary. Mary's spiritual life was perfectly centered in Jesus as she went with Christ to the Father in the Holy Spirit.

As the words of Vatican II tell us, Mary cooperated with Jesus in His redemptive effort. Throughout much of the time she was physically present to Him. At those times when she was not at His side, she was united with Him through a profound spiritual union. She was totally dedicated to Him and to His cause. She was His first and perfect disciple. She loved Him with a devotion and an intensity beyond our full comprehension.

All of Mary's other God-given gifts flow from her divine motherhood—from the fact that she is the Mother of Jesus. Her Immaculate Conception, her fullness of grace, her freedom from actual sin, her perpetual virginity, her bodily Assumption into Heaven—these and all her other gifts flow from her divine maternity.

One of these gifts not yet mentioned is her role as our spiritual mother. Yes, because Mary is the Mother of Christ, she is also our mother. This is a marvelous and most consoling reality upon which to further reflect.

two

Mother At Our Side

Standing by the cross of Jesus were His mother and His mother's sister, Mary the wife of Clopas, and Mary of Magdala. When Jesus saw His mother and the disciple there whom He loved, He said to His mother, "Woman, behold, your son." Then He said to the disciple, "Behold, your mother." (Jn. 19:25-27).

"In an utterly singular way she cooperated by her obedience, faith, hope, and burning charity in the Savior's work of restoring supernatural life to souls. For this reason she is a mother to us in the order of grace." (*Vatican* II).[2]

Mary is the Mother of Jesus. She is also our Mother. The above words of Scripture and of the Second Vatican Council attest to this.

Jesus has given us Mary as our spiritual mother. As He hung upon the cross, Jesus told John to look upon Mary as his mother, this John who represents all of us. In His moment of deepest anguish and suffering, Jesus was thinking of us. As the indescribable physical pain racked His body from head to toe, as the unfathomable spiritual anguish penetrated to the depths of His Heart, Jesus was thinking of us. If we allow this scene to penetrate into our hearts, if we take the time to contemplate the depth of Jesus' and Mary's love for us as Their Hearts were

3

pierced with grief, we are truly overwhelmed with the magnificent greatness and tenderness of the scene. Jesus was proclaiming Mary to be Mother of the Redemption. He was telling us that Mary is Mother to all peoples.

The fact that Mary is our mother, the fact that she has such a powerful role to play in our salvation in no way detracts from the mediatorship of Christ. Vatican II states:

"We have but one Mediator, as we know from the words of the Apostle: "For there is one God, and one Mediator between God and men, himself man, Christ Jesus, who gave himself as ransom for all." (*1 Tim.* 2:5-6). The maternal duty of Mary toward men in no way obscures or diminishes this unique mediation of Christ, but rather shows its power. For all the saving influences of the Blessed Virgin on men originate, not from some inner necessity, but from the divine pleasure. They flow forth from the superabundance of the merits of Christ, rest on His mediation, depend entirely on it, and draw all their power from it. In no way do they impede the immediate union of the faithful with Christ. Rather they foster this union."[3]

In saying that Mary is our spiritual mother, we are saying that Mary is the mother of our Christ-life. What is this life? Can we define it?

At Baptism the Persons of the Trinity communicate so intimately to us that, as a result, they leave their imprint or image upon us. This Trinitarian image is our life of sanctifying grace. This life of grace is a created participation in God's life, and since this gift of grace is mediated by Christ in His humanity, this Trinitarian image also has a Christic aspect. Christ as man has shown us how to live a God-like existence. He has shown us how to live the life of grace. This life of grace we possess allows us to enjoy the special presence of Father, Son, and Holy Spirit. Truly, the divine Persons dwell within us. Whether we refer to this life as the Christ-life, the life of grace, life in the Holy Spirit, or by other names, we are referring to one and the same reality. This reality, again, is the Christic, Trinitarian image given us through the Trinitarian communication.

St. Paul speaks of our life of grace in terms of our being baptized into the depth and resurrection of Jesus (*Rom.* 6:1-11). Again, Jesus mediates our life of grace. He has shown us how to live a Christ-like existence. Since Jesus' paschal mystery of death-resurrection sums up His own human existence, so it sums up our own. This is what St. Paul is telling us. Paul tells us that we live our life of Baptism, our life of grace, by continually dying and rising with Jesus—rising to a greater share in Christ's resurrection. Indeed, we live resurrection now and here-after. Living death-resurrection involves all of our Christian activities. While not giving an all-inclusive list, we do include the following: the reading of Scripture, prayer, the performance of daily duties, the doing of penance, making sacrifices, our jobs, periods of rest and relaxation, sharing meals with loved ones, reception of the sacraments, and, especially, participation in the Eucharist which is both sacrifice and sacrament.

This is our glorious existence made possible by God's great love for us and a major truth of this glorious existence is the fact that Jesus has given us Mary as our spiritual mother. Mary is the Mother of our Christ-life. In her loving, maternal role, she cooperates with the Holy Spirit in forming Christ in us. Pope John Paul II tells us:

"The Church knows and teaches that all the
saving influences of the Blessed Virgin on mankind originate from the divine pleasure...This
saving influence is sustained by the Holy Spirit,
Who, just as He overshadowed the Virgin Mary
when He began in her the divine motherhood,
in a similar way constantly sustains her solici-
tude for the brothers and sisters of her Son."[4]

Mary our mother is ever with us, guiding us, teaching
us, caring for us, protecting us, loving us. With her maternal assistance we go to the Father through and with Christ
in the Holy Spirit.

Mary nourishes our growth in Christ with a very tender
and specialized love for each of us. She regards each of
us as a precious, unique individual. John Paul II again
speaks to us:

"Of the essence of motherhood is the fact that
it concerns the person. Motherhood always
establishes a unique and unrepeatable relationship between two people: between mother and
child and between child and mother. Even when
the same woman is the mother of many children, her personal relationship with each one of
them is of the very essence of motherhood. For
each child is generated in a unique and
unrepeatable way, and this is true both for the
mother and for the child."[4]

The Holy Father then applies these ideas to Mary and
us:

"It can be said that motherhood in the order
of grace preserves the analogy with what in the
order of nature characterizes the union between
mother and child. In the light of this fact it

becomes easier to understand why in Christ's testament on Golgotha, His Mother's new motherhood is expressed in the singular, in reference to one man. *Behold, your son."*[5]

This is the awesome and consoling truth—you and I are very precious to Mary. She loves us much more than we can ever fathom. It is our great privilege and responsibility to love her in return. She asks for this love, she asks for our trust. As we give our love and trust to our mother, she wants us to come to her at all times and in all circumstances.

Are we sorrowful, anxious, troubled? Let us go to Mary our mother and ask her to console us. Let us ask her for the grace to handle our sorrow, our anxieties, our troubles properly—according to God's will. In this way our suffering will bring us closer to Christ as it simultaneously allows us to contribute to the ongoing Christianization of the world.

Are we joyful, happy, basking in the glow of a goal successfully accomplished? Let us go to Mary and ask her to help us handle our joy, our happiness, our success as God intends. Let us petition her not to allow our joy to make us forgetful of God, our God Who is the source of all true joy, success, and happiness.

Are we finding it particularly difficult to follow Christ in the here-and-now? In child-like trust we can approach our mother. Let us ask her for the grace to realize that the following of Christ is not always easy—that at times being a follower of Christ challenges our courage in a special way. We can also ask Mary to help us realize that even at such difficult times, Christ's grace makes our burden relatively light. Jesus has told us:

*Come to me, all you who labor and are bur-
dened, and I will give you rest.
Take my yoke upon you and learn from me,
for I am meek and humble of heart; and you
will find rest for yourselves. For my yoke is easy,
and my burden light.* (*Mt.*11:28-30).

Are we finding it is particularly easy to follow Christ
in the here-and-now? Let us go to Mary and ask her for
the grace to remain humble. Let us beseech Mary to keep
us from being inflated with pride, and ask her to help
us realize that without Jesus we can do nothing.

Mary, then, asks for our complete trust. She wants us
always to seek shelter under her maternal mantle. She
invites us to come to her in all circumstances—whether
it be in joy or sorrow, success or failure, laughter or tears.
Mary wants us to share in her maternal wisdom so that
we may understand how to use our various experiences
to come closer to God in Christ. Sharing our lives with
Mary in this fashion, and on a consistent basis, requires
that we love her, that we trust her, that we surrender ourselves to her maternal love.

Help us, Mother Mary, to probe ever more deeply into
the depths of your love for us. Help us to realize more
and more that to be loved by you is to experience a sweet-
ness, a warmth, a tenderness, a serenity, a security, which
makes us cry out, ''O Mother, how good and loving you
are!''

three

Mary And Our Personal Uniqueness

"Of the essence of motherhood is the fact that it concerns the person. Motherhood always establishes a unique and unrepeatable relationship between two people: between mother and child and between child and mother. Even when the same woman is the mother of many children, her personal relationship with each one of them is of the very essence of motherhood...

"It can be said that motherhood 'in the order of grace' preserves the analogy with what 'in the order of nature' characterizes the union between mother and child." (Pope John Paul II).[6]

We have already used these words in the previous chapter. We repeat them here for the purpose of discussing the concept of personal uniqueness. Each of us is unique—a unique reflection of God. Out of each one's uniqueness flows a special God-given mission. Cardinal Newman observes: "Everyone who breathes, high and low, educated and ignorant, young and old, man and woman, has a mission, has a work. We are not sent into this world for nothing; we are not born at random...God sees every one of us; He creates every soul, He lodges it in a body, one by one, for a purpose." [7]

And as Pope John Paul tells us, we each have a unique relationship with Mary. She loves each one of us very dearly, each in his or her own uniqueness. She knows

9

each of us has the awesome privilege and responsibility of allowing Christ to live in and through this personal uniqueness. As Mary cooperates with the Holy Spirit in forming Christ in us, she works with the Spirit in assisting us to accomplish our personal mission in life.

Each day we can strive to accomplish our mission under Mary's maternal mantle. Let us each day entrust ourselves to Mary's Immaculate Heart and dwell within this most pure haven. Here we feel loved, safe, confident, courageous in our efforts to act that day as the Father wills. Dwelling within Mary's Heart, we face our daily challenge of working with Christ to lessen the world's evil and to promote its goodness. Aware of Mary's special and unique love for each of us, we are strengthened in our attempt to accomplish our God-given mission in all the various circumstances of life within the human condition. Amidst joy and sorrow, success and failure, acceptance and rejection, laughter and tears—amidst whatever comprises each day's existence—we should rest secure knowing Mary is Mother at our side.

We should not waste time bemoaning the fact that we do not possess this or that gift which another has in abundance. We have the gifts God intends for us. We have the gifts we need to accomplish our mission in life. Concentrate to develop these gifts for love of God and neighbor because how we use these gifts is what we will be judged on—not on the fact that we lacked this or that talent.

I cannot accomplish your mission in life. You cannot accomplish mine. Each of us has something to give to Christ, His Church, and His world which no other can contribute. Again, this is an awesome privilege and responsibility.

God has given us Mary so that she may assist us in

living out this privilege and responsibility and we should daily ask her for wisdom to grow in the understanding of all that our mission involves. We should also petition her for the courage not to shirk the responsibility, but joyously to embrace it for the greater glory of God. With her mother's sense of pride, she wants us to succeed in fulfilling God's plan for us. The more we entrust ourselves to her, the more she places us with Christ so that He may live in and through us to further Christianize the world.

Yes, the more we entrust ourselves to Mary our Mother, the more we will be able to live out the truth Cardinal Newman puts before us: "We are not sent into this world for nothing; we are not born at random...God sees every one of us; He creates every soul, He lodges it in a body, one by one, for a purpose."

four

God's Will—Our Guiding Principle

*When his parents saw him, they were astonished, and
his mother said to him, "Son, why have you done this
to us? Your father and I have been looking for you with
great anxiety." And he said to them, "Why were you
looking for me? Did you not know that I must be in my
Father's house?" But they did not understand what he
said to them. (Lk. 2:48-50).*

The above scene describes how Mary and Joseph found
Jesus in the temple after having been separated from Him.
As they were returning home after the Passover celebra-
tion, they realized Jesus was not with them, and returned
to Jerusalem to search for Him. The scene has various lessons for us concerning God's will.

With the Holy Family traveling in two separate groups
(Mary with one, Joseph with the other, and Jesus with
either from time to time), we understand how Mary and
Joseph could have received conflicting stories regarding
their Son's whereabouts. The Father's will may have been
made known to Jesus in such a way that the timing of
His response precluded alerting His parents to the change
in His plan. Whatever the details were, we can be assured
that there was no error made on the parts of Jesus, Mary,
or Joseph. We can base our trust in this on what we know
through faith—that Jesus would never have been disobe-
dient or thoughtless toward His parents, and that Mary

12

and Joseph could not possibly have been inept parents. Even so, as people who expect certain behaviors of children and parents, we can be unsettled by some unanswered questions presented. Yet, since this event is included in Sacred Scripture, we know it has tremendous value for us as the Word of God. We also know that obedience to God's will always works in the best interests of everyone concerned, even when it is not obvious, even for quite some time.

The scene reminds us of the guiding principle of Jesus' life—loving conformity to His Father's will. Although Mary and Joseph were returning home, in some way Jesus knew He was supposed to remain in the temple at this particular time. His course of action was no different in this instance than it had been in the past and would be in the future. His Father's will was made manifest, and He obeyed; His Father showed the way, and He followed. The Father's will was always Jesus' way, every day, in all matters. As followers of Jesus, His guiding principle must also be ours.

This event in Christ's life also demonstrates that conformity to God's will sometimes brings hurt or sorrow to loved ones. Jesus knew that His remaining behind would cause suffering for Mary and Joseph—we can well imagine their anxiety. Jesus was sorry this had to be. He certainly was not insensitive to His parent's feelings, yet He had to do what He did. There can be similar situations in our own lives. Precisely because we are striving to seek out and do God's will, we may be causing hurt to loved ones. We know, however, there is no other course of action if we are to be open to God's designs for us.

The finding of the child Jesus in the temple illustrates still a further point regarding conformity to God's will. Mary and Joseph knew that somehow it was God's will that Jesus remain in Jerusalem as they themselves headed back to Nazareth. Yet they did not comprehend why all this happened. They recognized God's will, but they did not understand it. They accepted this will, however, along with the pain it produced in their lives.

The application of this lesson to our own Christian lives is vividly manifest. At times there occurs an incident we do not understand. We realize that somehow this is God's will, at least His permissive will, yet we do not understand why, and our unknowning is part of our pain.

Mary always perfectly conformed herself in love to God's will. It was her joy to so act. Sometimes the doing of God's will caused her considerable suffering, as we see from the above Gospel scene. Later on, the sword of suffering would pierce her even more deeply.

In summary, we can say that Mary always reached out and embraced God's will with the deepest love, whether this was easy or very difficult. Mary has left us these famous words: *Behold, I am the handmaid of the Lord. May it be done to me according to your word.* (*Lk.* 1:38). Let us ask our mother to obtain for us the grace to grow in our own conformity to the will of God.

five

Consecration To Christ And Mary

"If, in the strict sense in question here, consecration makes one belong to God—how is it possible to speak of consecrating oneself to Mary? It is possible because by God's will Mary has something to do with our Christian life, with our sanctification. She is certainly not, like Christ, the source of salvation but she is maternally ordered to our life as children of God—always, however, in perfect union with her Son and subordinate to Him...Hence, in the full sense of the word a consecration to Mary includes...a real and essential reference to Christ and to the Baptism that binds us to Him." (A. Bossard).[8]

Before we can intelligently discuss consecration to Christ and Mary we must understand the basic concept of consecration in the overall context of the Christian life.

To consecrate means to make sacred, to make holy. Only God can make a being holy. So to speak of our consecration is to speak of God's activity in making us holy— His activity of giving us a share in His own holiness. At Baptism—we receive a share in God's life—a share in His holiness. Christ is the mediator of this grace-life. We are baptized into Christ, into His death and resurrection. In Baptism we become holy by sharing in the holiness of Christ. We become consecrated, sealed with the divine

15

holiness. We belong to the Father, through Christ in the Holy Spirit.

On our part, we must respond to God's consecration of us. We must live out the consecration of Baptism. We must realize what God has done for us in Christ and live according to this awareness. We need to live the life of holiness and grow in it. In other words, we must develop the life of grace, the Christ-life. We are given the gift, but we must respond.

What God has done for us in Christ involves Mary. God has given us a Christ-life, our life of grace, and Mary is the Mother of this Christ-life. Consequently, living out our life of consecration to God—living out the Christ-life—includes allowing Mary to increasingly be the Mother of our Christ-life.

Consecration to Mary, therefore, is an aspect of our consecration to God in Christ. It is entrusting ourselves entirely to her maternal love so that she can bring us closer to Jesus—so that we can increasingly live out our consecration to God in Christ.

At Fatima, Our Lady asked that we consecrate ourselves to her Immaculate Heart. Mary shows us her heart as symbol of her love for God and us. She asks us to make a return of love to her—to consecrate ourselves to her. She wants us to entrust ourselves to her completely so that she may help us love God and neighbor. Her heart, symbol of her own great love of God and the human race, is a model for us in our own strivings to love God and neighbor.

As stated above, consecration to Mary is an aspect of our consecration to God in Christ and she has asked for consecration to her Immaculate Heart so that she may assist us. Christ, in turn, invites us to live out this consecration to Him through consecration to His Heart. We see the divine symmetry—consecration to the Immaculate Heart helps us live out our consecration to Christ Who reveals His Heart to us as symbol of His love. His heart also asks for our own return of love. We see, then, the most intimate link between consecration to the Immaculate Heart and consecration to the Sacred Heart.

Pope Pius XII reminds us of this union: "That grace for the Christian family and for the whole human race may flow more abundantly from devotion to the Sacred Heart, let the faithful strive to join it closely with devotion to the Immaculate Heart of the Mother of God."[9]

Archbishop R. Arulappa, one very much interested in devotion to Mary's Immaculate Heart, reminds us that Our Lord Himself has let it be known that He wishes devotion to the Immaculate Heart to be united with devotion to His Sacred Heart.

The Archbishop says:

> "In connection with the apparitions of Our Lady at Fatima, Sister Lucia, one of the seers still alive, has been saying that on June 13, 1929 Our Lady requested, (as the sister herself records in *'Memoirs and Letters of Sister Lucia,'* published in 1973), as follows: 'The Good Lord promises to end the persecution in Russia, if the Holy Father will himself make a solemn act of reparation and consecration of Russia...as well as ordering all the Bishops of the Catholic world to do the same.'
>
> "On March 21st, 1982, Sister Lucia further explained to the Apostolic Nuncio, and two other witnesses, that the Pope must select a date on which to order the Bishops of the whole world to make a solemn act of reparation and

consecration of Russia to the most Sacred Hearts
of Jesus and Mary, each in his own Cathedral
and at the same time as the act effected by the
Pope.

"There are actually two versions of the vision
of Our Lady on June 13th 1929, but they are
essentially the same. In the better known ver-
sion, Our Lady says: 'The moment has come for
God to ask the Holy Father to make, in union
with all the Bishops of the world, the consecration of Russia to my Immaculate Heart. He
promises to save Russia by these means.' The
special mention of 'Russia' in this Act of Consecration is to be noted.

"When Sister Lucia asked our Lord why He
would not convert Russia without such an act
of Consecration. He replied: 'Because I want my
whole Church to recognize this consecration as
a triumph of the Immaculate Heart of Mary, so
as to extend its cult later on, and to place devotion to this Immaculate Heart beside the devotion to my Sacred Heart.' "[10]

Has this act of consecration, requested by Mary and
Christ, occurred? In a message given to Fr. Don Stefano
Gobbi, on March 25, 1984, the very day of the consecration which some think fulfilled the collegial act of consecration requested by Our Lady, Mary reportedly stated:

*Before all I ask it of Pope John Paul II, the first
of my beloved sons, whom on the occasion of
this feast, performed the consecration in a sol-
emn manner, after writing to the bishops of the
world and inviting them to do so in union with
him.*

Unfortunately the invitation was not wel-comed by all the bishops; particular circum-stances have not yet permitted the explicit consecration of Russia which I have requested many times. As I have already told you, this consecration will be made to me when the bloody events are well on the way to actuality. (Fr. Gobbi, #287).[11]

Fr. Gobbi, who is spiritual director of the *Marian Movement of Priests* and a frequent receiver of Marian locutions, received another message from Mary on May 13, 1990. In this message Our Lady again states that the collegial act of consecration has not yet been made:

Russia has not been consecrated to me by the Pope together with all the bishops and thus she has not received the grace of conversion and has spread her errors throughout the world, provoking wars, violence, bloody revolutions and persecutions of the Church and of the Holy Father. (Fr. Gobbi, #425).

Pope John Paul II himself evidently realized, after inviting all the bishops to make the 1984 consecration with him, that the specific act of consecration requested by Mary was still to be fulfilled. After his own act of consecration of the world to Mary, and in words addressed to Our Lady of Fatima in St. Peter's Basilica, the Holy Father said: "We wished to choose this Sunday for the act of entrusting and consecration of the world . . .of all peoples especially those who have a very great need of this consecration and entrustment, of those peoples for whom You Yourself are awaiting our act of consecration."[12]

When will this specific act of consecration requested by Our Lady and Christ occur? Sr. Lucia gives us the answer: According to Sr. Lucy, God will permit the grace of the collegial consecration only "when a sufficient number are complying with the message of Fatima."[13]

We see, then, how extremely important it is for each of us to live the message of Fatima. If we are consecrated to her Immaculate Heart, we certainly want to do what Mary asks of us, and Mary's Fatima requests include: 1) penance 2) the daily recitation of the Rosary, 3) the five First Saturdays, 4) consecration to the Immaculate Heart.[14] Following is a brief commentary on each of these:

. . . **Penance** is the turning away from sin, asking pardon for sin—which, of course, includes sorrow for sin—and making reparation to the Hearts of Jesus and Mary for the offenses committed against them. The spirit of reparation should be present in all we do in Christ—including performance of daily duties. We should include in our activities the practice of fasting, a practice requested by Our Lady at Medjugorje. As we perform our activities in union with Christ and Mary, we are encouraged to say the Fatima prayer: "O my Jesus, I offer this for love of Thee, for the conversion of poor sinners, and in reparation for all the sins committed against the Immaculate Heart of Mary."

. . .Our Lady of Fatima also requested daily recitation of the **Rosary**. The rosary is one of Mary's favorite forms of prayer. The power of the rosary has been proven countless times over the centuries. The promises Mary gave to St. Dominic and Blessed Alan concerning those who say the rosary are truly remarkable. The Fatima prayer to be said after each decade of the rosary is: "O my Jesus, forgive us our sins, save us from the fire of Hell, lead all souls to Heaven, especially those who have most need of Thy mercy.''[15]

. . .The practice of the **five first Saturdays** involves: 1) Going to confession, which may be done from 8 days before to 8 days after the first Saturday. Of course, if a person is in the state of serious sin, the confession must be made before receiving communion. 2) Receiving Holy Communion. 3) Recitation of 5 decades of the rosary. 4) Meditating for 15 minutes on the mysteries of the rosary. All of the above (except confession) must be done on the first Saturday of 5 consecutive months with the intention of making reparation to the Immaculate Heart. For those who make the five first Saturdays, Our Lady of Fatima has promised to assist them at the hour of death with all the graces necessary for salvation.

. . .Another request of Our Lady of Fatima—one which includes all the others— is that we **consecrate** ourselves to her Immaculate Heart. What this consecration means we have stated earlier. Simply put, we can say that in consecrating ourselves to Mary we give and entrust ourselves to her so that she may bring us ever closer to the Heart of Christ, this Christ Who brings us to the Father in the Holy Spirit. This act of consecration obviously includes our willingness to observe the other requests of Our Lady of Fatima.

A great sign of our consecration to the Immaculate Heart is the wearing of the Brown Scapular. Sister Lucia has said that all Catholics should wear the Brown Scapular as part of the Fatima message. She said, *The Rosary and the Scapular are inseparable.* . .In 1251, when she gave the Scapular to St. Simon Stock and thereby to the world, the Queen of Heaven stated: *Whosoever dies clothed in this shall never suffer eternal fire.* Wearing the Scapular serves as a constant reminder of one's personal consecration to Mary and of the necessity of imitating her virtues and heeding her requests."[16] Only priests properly authorized can validly enroll one in the Brown Scapular.

We can extend this connection between consecration to the Immaculate Heart and consecration to the Heart of Christ. In a message to Don Stefano Gobbi, Mary says, *In my Immaculate Heart the Son assimilates you to make you more completely resemble Himself, and to associate you with His own life. It is in my heavenly garden that the wonder of your transformation takes place.* (Fr. Gobbi, #266).

Mary, then, tells us that consecration to her Immaculate Heart leads us to an even greater assimilation to Christ, to a deeper living out of our consecration to Christ. In the Immaculate Heart we are increasingly formed into the likeness of Christ. We are increasingly drawn into the Heart of Christ and more and more transformed in Him.

St. Louis de Montfort in his own way tells us of the connection between our life in Mary and our life in Christ: "The Holy Spirit espoused Mary and produced His greatest work, the Incarnate Word, in her, by her, and through her. He has never disowned her and so He continues to produce everyday, in a mysterious but real manner, the souls of the elect in her and through her. . .Since Mary produced the head of the elect, Jesus Christ, she must also produce the members of that head, that is, all true Christians."[17]

In the above quoted message of Mary to Fr. Gobbi, Mary says that in her Heart, "the Son assimilates you to make you more and more completely resemble Himself, and to associate you with His own life." Karl Rahner, one of the greater theologians of our times, speaks to us about this association with Christ's life: "We can only get a complete picture of Christian existence, such as it is given by God and such as we should make it, if we take a good look at the whole life of Christ." Further on, Rahner reminds us that Jesus still retains the mysteries or events of His past existence: "Jesus has not lost a thing. He has not only saved His physical being intact, but everything has remained present, as it were, in its hidden, sublime essence." Finally, Rahner tells us that through our union with Christ we relive His mysteries: "In other words, just as His cross and the totality of His life have become part of our life, so also is His Resurrection a factor in our present existence." [18]

To end our reflection on consecration to the Hearts of Jesus and Mary, we might consider what Our Lady of Fatima said to Jacinta:

> *Tell everybody that God gives graces through the Immaculate Heart of Mary. Tell them to ask graces from her, and that the Heart of Jesus wishes to be venerated together with the Immaculate Heart of Mary. Ask them to plead for peace from the Immaculate Heart of Mary, for the Lord has confided the peace of the world to her.* [19]

six

Fatima: Call Of The Immaculate Heart

God wishes you to remain in the world for some time because He wants to use you to establish in the world the devotion to my Immaculate Heart. I promise salvation to those who embrace it, and their souls will be loved by God as flowers placed by myself to adorn His throne. (Our Lady of Fatima to Lucia.)[20]

In the previous chapter we made numerous references to Fatima. Let's review the events that happened there.

Fatima is situated in Portugal, not too far from the city of Lisbon. The terrain of Fatima is hilly with numerous cedar trees lining the valleys and the hills.

In 1917, the Blessed Virgin Mary appeared to three small shepherd children, Lucia dos Santos and her cousins Jacinta and Francisco Marto. She appeared to them on six occasions from May to October. With one exception, Mary always appeared on the 13th of the month above an oak tree in the Cova da Iria. The lone exception occurred in August. During this particular month Mary appeared to the children on the 19th near Valinhos. The three had been imprisoned by the civil authorities and were thus prevented from being in the Cova da Iria for the customary apparition on the 13th.

The message which Mary gave to the children has been called her peace plan. We have given a brief description of Mary's Fatima message in the previous chapter.

Among the requests of Our Lady of Fatima is the call for consecration to her Immaculate Heart. This is her key request—all her other requests are contained in this central one. This is obvious from a reflection on what consecration to the Immaculate Heart means. It means that we completely entrust ourselves to Mary so that we may completely belong to Christ. If we thus give ourselves completely to Mary, it is obvious we are willing to fulfill the other requests she has made at Fatima.

It is extremely important that we live the Fatima message through consecration to the Immaculate Heart. As stated earlier, Sr. Lucia has said that the particular act of consecration of Russia to the Immaculate Heart which Mary has requested—with the conversion of Russia and world peace to follow—will not occur until a sufficient number of people are living the Fatima message. Since the Fatima message is centered in consecration to the Immaculate Heart, we see the overwhelming importance of making this consecration. (Contrary to what some believe, Russia has *not* realized complete conversion).

The Immaculate Heart has drawn millions and millions of pilgrims to Fatima. To be there, especially on the 13th of the above mentioned months, is a very special experience. I was privileged to be at Fatima on October 13th, 1992, for the 75th anniversary of Mary's last apparition to the three children—the apparition attested to by the great miracle of the sun.

On this occasion there was the usual candlelight rosary procession on the eve of the 13th. On this crisp, cool October night there were hundreds of thousands of pilgrims in the great square in front of the Basilica. Their reverence and devotion was most obvious and most inspiring.

The next day was a bright, sunny day with clear blue

sky—a gift of Mary, the Woman clothed with the sun: *A great sign appeared in the sky, a woman clothed with the sun, with the moon under her feet, and on her head a crown of twelve stars. (Rev.* 12:1). There were even more pilgrims present for the morning outdoor Mass than had been on hand the previous evening. One estimate placed the crowd at one million. Whatever the actual number, the devotion of the pilgrims was even more impressive than their numbers. For over three hours the services continued. Throughout there was reverence and deep devotion evident. Although many of the pilgrims were Portuguese, there were also people present from numerous other countries. Despite the length of the services, despite the hundreds of thousands filling the square, there was this ongoing and pervasive silence. It was one of the most extraordinary events I have ever witnessed.

One of the highlights of the services was the procession—before Mass—of the Our Lady of Fatima statue from the Apparitions Chapel to the outdoor altar in front of the Basilica, and the statue's return procession after Mass. The pilgrims' deep devotion to Our Lady of Fatima was very evident during these processions.

While I was at Fatima, whenever I would visit the Apparitions Chapel—built on the site of Mary's apparitions to Lucia, Jacinta, and Francisco—there were numerous pilgrims praying. Often there would be a Mass taking place. At other times the pilgrims would simply be praying with deep devotion before the statue of Our Lady of Fatima which is enclosed in glass within the sanctuary. Leading down to the Chapel of Apparitions from the far end of the square—a distance of about 100 yards—lies a special pathway. Along this path certain pilgrims, in an act of sacrifice, walk on their knees until they arrive at the Chapel.

Pilgrims also flock to the Basilica to attend Masses, to

engage in private prayer, and to visit the crypts of Jacinta and Francisco. Their remains lie in the front of the Church. Those of Jacinta, to the left; those of Francisco, to the right. As one observes the pilgrims praying at the crypt sites, one can speculate on what goes through their minds. Certainly some must be in awe at the wonders God has worked through these two small shepherd children: *"I give praise to you, Father, Lord of heaven and earth, for although you have hidden these things from the wise and the learned you have revealed them to the childlike."* (*Mt.* 11:25).

Fatima is an attraction for millions. The Heart of a mother, the loving Heart of your mother and my mother is what attracts. Yet, the attraction of Fatima does not stop at Mary. At Fatima—as she always does—Mary points to her Son, Jesus. The center of attention at Fatima is the Eucharistic Heart of Jesus and all devotions lead to the Mass. Symbolizing all this is the statue of the Sacred Heart which stands high upon its pedestal in the center of the great square. The figure of Christ stands with outstretched arms, welcoming all to come closer to His Heart. Our Lady of Fatima, in her motherly love for us, is ever so eager to lead us to this Heart of her Son. At Fatima, then, we are drawn to two Hearts: *In my Immaculate Heart the Son assimilates you to make you more completely resemble Himself, and to associate you with His own life. It is in my heavenly garden that the wonder of your own transformation takes place.* (Fr. Gobbi, #266).

seven

Being Led By Jesus And Mary

...Why do you become troubled? Why are you worried? To be consecrated to me means to let yourself be led by me. It means to entrust yourself to me, like a child who lets itself be led by its mother. (Message of Mary to Fr. Gobbi #6).

One of the most difficult tasks in the spiritual life is to engage in the process of letting go. There is something in us which wants to remain in control. We must remember, however, that growth in the spiritual life means increased abandonment to God in Christ.

God has given us Mary as our spiritual mother to help us grow in abandonment. As we more and more entrust ourselves to the Immaculate Heart, Mary increasingly aids in leading us to closer union with the Heart of Christ—to an increased abandonment to Christ.

We have to have goals in the spiritual life. We have to schedule our spiritual exercises. We have to make plans for our ministry—for our services to others in the Lord. We must plan to try to make the best use of our time.

But we must do these things with the overall attitude of allowing Christ and Mary to guide us in the Spirit. We make plans with the understanding that Christian prudence asks this of us. We do not map things out in order to be in control in a way which goes against entrusting ourselves to Christ and Mary. When it becomes clear that Christ and our Mother want us to make changes in what we have planned, we must ask for the grace to be spiritually free—to once again abandon ourselves to Jesus and Mary and allow Them to lead us anew in the Holy Spirit.

Our consecration to Christ and Mary means that we always strive to entrust ourselves totally to Them. And as we grow in this spirit of entrustment, we grow in the realization of what it means to be led by Jesus and Mary in the Spirit. We also grow in the desire to be so led.

In words to one of His chosen ones, Jesus speaks about the need for this spirit of abandonment:

"My people need to surrender their control to Me. I will then be able to fill them with My radiance. This is also part of obedience. The most difficult thing for My people to do is to give Me their control! They are afraid they will lose their power. How can I express the seriousness of this lesson on control?

"By trying to hold on to power, they will lose it, because they are grasping the wrong source of power. By surrendering your control, you shall be gaining My control! Being afraid of following My ways because of the need to surrender control, is an emotion placed in you by the evil one!

"So trust in Me when I say to surrender unto Me with an open heart. You will gain control...MY CONTROL...and you shall never fear again. You will only be filled with My goodness, My happiness, My mercy, My power, My love and My peace!"[21]

eight

Mary's Teaching At Medjugorje

Dear children! Today I invite you to holiness. You cannot live without holiness. Consequently, overcome all sin with love. Overcome every difficulty you meet with love. Dear children, I beg you to live love within yourselves. Thank you for your response to my call. (Message of Mary at Medjugorje, July 10, 1986).[22]

I am beginning to write this particular chapter as I am actually present here in Medjugorje. Our group may have set a record for length of time in arriving here. But pilgrimages usually have their share of inconveniences, and the length of travel time happened to be one of ours. Obviously, the many rewards of making a pilgrimage far outweigh the inconveniences involved.

In my brief treatment of Medjugorje, I am going to concentrate on the spiritual teaching which Mary has been giving through her message with only a few remarks concerning the historical background of the events.[23]

This chapter on Medjugorje follows closely my treatment of Mary's message at Fatima. This is by design. I hope to show that there is a close connection between Our Lady's teaching at Fatima and that at Medjugorje.

A very brief background on the events at Medjugorje is appropriate before discussing Mary's teaching as contained in the messages. The official Church investigation regarding the authenticity of the Medjugorje apparitions

30

and messages is an ongoing one. No final declaration has yet been made and we submit to the final decision of the Church in the matter. Mary first appeared at Medjugorje on June 24, 1981. The following day marks the first time Our Lady actually spoke with the six young visionaries, and she has asked that this date, June 25, be observed as the anniversary date of Our Lady of Medjugorje. The names of the visionaries are: Mirjana Dragicevic Soldo, Ivanka Ivankovic Elez, Jakov Colo, Ivan Dragicevic, Marija Pavlovic, Vicka Ivankovic.

The first apparitions occurred on Mt. Podbrdo, which is about a twenty minute walk from St. James church. The church itself has long since become the main scene for the apparitions.

Millions of pilgrims have climbed Mt. Podbrdo, or "Apparition Hill," as it is often called. It is a rather steep climb up a very rocky path. Upon reaching the site of the apparitions, one can see for miles across the Medjugorje valley which is surrounded by mountains. A key spot in this panoramic view is St. James church. As one looks out on the scene below, there is a definite impression of quiet and peace. This is only to be expected in a locale which Mary has chosen to appear so many, many times, this Mary who is Queen of Peace. In this far off place, a place far removed from the events and activities which the world considers to be important, Mary has chosen to appear to six of her little ones. Through them she has been delivering a message which is destined to change the world—a message which is aimed at making God central in the lives of all those who will listen to her pleadings. Through six young visionaries in a village of 2,000 to 3,000 inhabitants, Mary is accomplishing all this.

Our group had the privilege of meeting Ivan and Vicka, two of the visionaries. We also were very privileged to be in the choir loft of the church on January 1, 1993, when

Ivan received his daily apparition from Our Blessed Mother. It lasted for about seven minutes.

Vicka addressed our group in front of her home—also through an interpreter. She is a very gracious person, smiling most of the time. After she talked to us regarding Our Lady's messages for about fifteen minutes, she invited us to approach her two by two. She placed one hand on each pilgrim and prayed over each set of two pilgrims for about one minute.

We also had the privilege of meeting with Jelena Vasilj, a young lady of about twenty who is a resident of Medjugorje. She has been receiving locutions or messages from Mary and Jesus since she was ten years old. If I remember correctly, she said that at first it was Mary who spoke to her, but now it is, for the most part, Jesus Who gives her messages. She told us that she has never received apparitions. She speaks English well. It was a pleasure to be able to dialogue directly with her. I was very impressed with her knowledge of the spiritual life.

A summary of Mary's messages at Medjugorje would be as follows: 1) love's call to conversion; 2) faith, hope, and love; 3) the Mass; 4) the sacrament of reconciliation; 5) prayer; 6) the reading of Scripture; 7) fasting and other forms of sacrifice; 8) peace; 9) consecration to the Heart of Christ and to the Immaculate Heart of Mary.

Love's Call to Conversion

A very fundamental message of Medjugorje is that God and Mary love us. In her March 25, 1988, message Mary tells us:

> *Dear children, today, also I am inviting you to complete surrender to God. Dear children, you are not conscious of how God loves you with such a great love. . .*

Speaking of her own love for us, Mary says in the November 20, 1986 message:

> *Dear children! Today, also, I am calling you to love and to pay attention with a special love to all the messages I am giving you. God does not want you lukewarm and indecisive, but totally committed to Him. You know that I love you and that I am burning out of love for you...*

In their great love for us, God and Mary call us to conversion. Mary tells us:

> *Dear children, today, again I am calling you to complete conversion...I am inviting you, dear children to convert fully to God.* (January 25, 1988).

There are two basic types of conversion. One type is that experienced by one who has been on the wrong path and accepts the call to come back to God. The second type applies to those who are in a basically good relationship with God, but realize the necessity of deepening this bond. This is a lifelong process. Ivan told us that we all are in need of change—we all fall under one or the other of the two types of conversion. And Vicka reminded us of what Mary says above—that Mary calls us to complete conversion. This is another way of saying that Mary calls us to the highest holiness. This is the purpose of her messages, and why this chapter begins with a message of Mary calling us to this holiness.

Faith, Hope and Love

To grow in the life of conversion—the life of holiness— is to grow in faith, hope, and love. These are the three most important Christian virtues. As we develop these virtues, we grow in the Christ-life, a life of grace, the life of holiness. Mary tells us:

> *. . .Therefore, little children, believe and pray that the Father increase your faith, and then ask for whatever you need. I am with you and I am rejoicing because of your conversion and I am protecting you with my motherly mantle. Thank you for having responded to my call.* (April 25, 1988).

The virtue of hope allows us to desire God, to want to live according to His plan for us. Hope also enables us to trust that God will assist us to live in this manner. Trust aids us in abandoning ourselves increasingly to Mary and to God. Growth in trust is extremely important for growth in the life of holiness. Mary talks to us about this growth in trust:

> *Dear children, I invite you to prayer now when Satan is strong and wishes to make as many souls as possible his own. Pray, dear children, and have more trust in me, because I am here in order to help you, and to guide you on a new path toward a new life. Therefore, dear little children, listen and live what I tell you, because it is important for you, when I shall not be with you any longer, that you remember my words and all which I told you. I call you to begin to change your life from the beginning and that you decide for conversion not with words but with your life. Thank you for having responded to my call.* (October 25, 1992).

Love is the most important of all the virtues. Ivan reminded us that the messages of love are among Mary's most important messages. Indeed, she often speaks about love.

> *Children! You do not know how to love and you do not know how to listen with love to the words I am giving you. Be aware... that I am your mother and that I have come to the Earth to teach you how to listen out of love, how to pray out of love...* (November 29, 1984).

> *Dear children! You know that the day of joy is coming near, but without love you will attain nothing...* (December 13, 1984).

> *Dear children! Today I call you to live the word this week. 'I love God!' Dear children, with love you will achieve everything, and even what you think is impossible.* (February 28, 1985).

The Eucharistic Sacrifice

Vicka related that Mary tells us that the Mass marks the holiest time of our lives. The Mass is the center of our lives. The Mass is our chief source for growth in the life of conversion and a life of holiness. In the Eucharistic sacrifice we offer ourselves to the Father with and through Christ in the Holy Spirit, with Mary our Mother at our side.

In the Eucharistic offering, Christ gives Himself to us and we give ourselves to Him. We need to take the time to reflect upon the awesomeness of this gift of the Lord Jesus. He gives Himself to us—body, blood, soul, and divinity. What an amazing, beautiful, and total giving!

The Christ Who suffered excruciating pain upon the cross, the Christ Who with lacerated body hung in agony and love, the Christ Who had His Heart pierced with a lance—this is the same Christ Who continues to give Himself completely to us in the Eucharist. What is our appreciation of this tremendous gift? Do we spend sufficient time in silent communication with Jesus after receiving the Eucharist? Do we sufficiently realize that Jesus' total gift of Himself calls for the total gift of ourselves to Him?

Mary speaks to us about the Mass:

> *Dear children, I wish to call you to live the Holy Mass. There are many of you who have experienced the beauty of the Mass but there are some who come unwillingly. I have chosen you dear children and Jesus is giving you His graces in the Holy Mass. Therefore, consciously live the Holy Mass. Let every coming to Holy Mass be joyful. Come with love and accept the Holy Mass. Thank you for your response to my call.* (April 3, 1986).

> *Dear children, God wants to make you holy. Therefore through me He invites you to complete surrender. Let Holy Mass be your life. Understand that Church is God's palace, the place in which I gather you and want to show you the way to God. Come and pray. Neither look at others nor slander them, but rather, let your life be a testimony on the way of holiness. Churches deserve respect and are set apart as holy because God Who became man dwells in them day and night.* (April 25, 1988).

The Sacrament of Reconciliation

Our life of ongoing conversion—our life of holiness—profits greatly from frequent confession. Mary tell us:

Dear children! Today I wish to call you to Confession... (March 24, 1985).

Mary invites us to go to confession at least once a month. Through frequent confession we become more sensitive regarding the ways we offend God. We receive strength to work against those failings which hinder our growth in Christ. We should make our confessions in peace, and through them, be led to even greater peace.

Prayer

The visionaries of Medjugorje all emphasize the great importance of prayer in our lives. The word "pray" occurs so very frequently in Our Lady's messages. Mary is constantly reminding us that prayer is extremely crucial in our process of conversion as well as for peace to come to the world.

The Mass is the greatest prayer. The more we prayerfully participate in the Mass, the more profit we derive for ourselves and others.

But it is not only a prayerful attitude at Mass which is important. We must also pray at other times and this prayer outside of the Mass is extremely important regarding our participation in the Eucharistic sacrifice. Such prayer can prepare us for participating in the Mass in an ever deeper fashion, and help us live the Mass as we leave the altar of God and go to the various activities of our daily lives.

We must live a life of consistent prayer. We should not become discouraged when we find prayer difficult, or when we seem to be praying so poorly, when distractions and other difficulties plague us during prayer. Prayer requires perseverance. So let us ask Jesus and Mary to help us pray, to help us increasingly realize the extreme importance of prayer for ourselves and others. Let us always remember that Our Lady of Fatima has said that many souls go to Hell because there is no one to pray and make sacrifices for them. At Medjugorje Mary constantly speaks of prayer:

Dear children, today like never before I invite you to prayer. Your prayer should be a prayer for peace. Satan is strong and wishes not only to destroy human life, but also nature and the planet on which you live. Therefore, dear children, pray that you can protect yourselves through prayer with the blessing of God's peace. God sent me to you so that I can help you. If you wish to, grasp the rosary. The rosary alone can do miracles in the world and in your lives. I bless you and I stay among you as long as it is God's will. Thank you that you will not betray my presence here and I thank you because your response is serving God and peace. Thank you for having responded to my call. (January 25, 1991).

Dear children, I call you to prayer. By means of prayer, little children, you obtain joy and peace. Through prayer you are richer in the mercy of God. Therefore, little children, let prayer be the life of each one of you. Especially I call you to pray so that all of those who are far away from God will be converted. Then all hearts will be richer because God will rule in the hearts of all men. Therefore little children, pray, pray, pray. Let prayer begin to rule in the whole world. Thank you for having responded to my call. (August 25, 1989).

The Reading of Scripture

Reading Scripture, especially the Gospels, is an excellent source for growing in the knowledge of Christ. If we wish to turn to God more and more—if we wish to pursue the challenge of conversion, turning to Scripture is essential. By knowing Jesus more intimately through the Gospels, we can follow Him more closely as He leads us along the path of ongoing conversion to a deeper union with the Father in the Holy Spirit with Mary our Mother at our side.

Included in Mary's remarks on Scripture is her telling us to live the message of *Matthew* 6:24-34 in which we are told not to worry about tomorrow and that we cannot serve God and money. Here is another message of Mary concerning Scripture:

[Tenth Anniversary.] *Dear children, today on this great day which you have given to me, I desire to bless all of you and to say, 'These days while I am with you are days of grace.' I desire to teach you and to help you walk on the path of holiness. There are many people who do not desire to understand my messages and to accept with seriousness what I am saying. But you are therefore called and asked, that by your life and daily living, you witness my presence. If you pray, God will help you discover the true reason for my coming. Therefore little children, pray and read the Sacred Scriptures so that through my coming you discover the message of Sacred*

Scripture for you. Thank you for having responded to my call. (June 25, 1991).

Fasting and Other Forms of Sacrifice

The quest for holiness, the quest for continuing conversion, includes carrying the cross. We are baptized into Christ's death-resurrection as St. Paul tells us (*Rom.* 6:1-11). As Christ embraced the cross to give us new life—a share in His resurrection—so must we also bear the cross in order to grow in the Christ-life ourselves and to help others experience the life Jesus came to give. Mary speaks to us about the place of the cross in our lives.

Dear children! The second message for Lenten Days is that you renew your prayer before the cross. Dear children, I am giving you special graces and Jesus is giving you special graces from the cross. Accept them and live them. Reflect on Jesus' passion and unite yourselves to Jesus in life. Thank you for your response to my call. (February 20, 1986).

One form of the cross is the practice of fasting. Mary has asked for this at Medjugorje:

Dear children! Today again I am calling you to prayer and fasting. You know, dear children with your help I can do everything and force Satan not to seduce people to evil and to remove him from this place. Satan, dear people, watches for every individual. He wants particularly to bring confusion to every one of you. Dear children, I ask that your every day become prayer and complete surrender to God. Thank you for your response to my call. (September 4, 1986).

As we are able, Mary asks us to fast on bread and water every Wednesday and Friday. For those who are unable to do this, they should fast in their own way. She also requests other forms of sacrifice:

> *Dear children! I invite you to prayer so that with your prayers you will help Jesus to realize all plans that are here. By offerings and sacrifices to Jesus everything will be fulfilled that is planned. Satan cannot do anything. Thank you for your response to my call.* (January 9, 1986).

Peace

During my visit to Medjugorje Ivan and Vicka spoke to us, and stressed the very important role peace plays in Mary's teaching. The further we progress along the path of conversion the more we experience the peace of Christ. The more we possess the peace of Christ, the more capable we are of helping to give peace to the world. The Queen of Peace stated:

> *Dear children, through your own peace, I am calling you to help others to see and to start searching for peace. Dear children, you are at peace and therefore, you cannot comprehend the absence of peace. Again, I am calling you so that through prayer and your life you will help destroy everything evil in people and uncover the deception which Satan is using. Pray for truth to prevail in every heart. Thank you for your response to my call.* (September 23, 1986).

Consecration

In Mary's teachings at Medjugorje, consecration to the Heart of Jesus and to her own Immaculate Heart play a vital role:

> *Dear children, my invitation that you live the messages which I am giving you, is a daily one. Especially, little children, because I want to draw you closer to the Heart of Jesus. Therefore, little children, I am inviting you to consecration to Jesus, My dear Son, so that each of your hearts may be His. And then, I am inviting you to consecration to my Immaculate Heart. I want you to consecrate yourselves as persons, as families, and as parishes, so that all belongs to God through my hands. Therefore, dear little children, pray that you may comprehend the greatness of this message which I am giving you. I do not want anything for myself, rather, all for the salvation of your souls. Satan is strong and therefore, you, little children press tight against My Motherly Heart. Thank you for having responded to my call.* (October 25, 1988).

There are two points concerning this message which I would like to emphasize. First, notice the connection Mary makes between living the messages and consecration to the Heart of Jesus through her own Immaculate Heart. Secondly, notice the great importance Mary attaches to this particular message. She says to us:

> *Therefore, little children, pray that you may comprehend the greatness of this message which I am giving you.*

Indeed, Mary is telling us that this particular message is an extremely critical one, an extremely pivotal one. Our mother is telling us that all her messages are connected with consecration to the Hearts of Jesus and Mary. In a later message, Mary again emphasizes the central position in her teaching of her call to consecration to the Heart of Christ and to her own Immaculate Heart:

Dear children! Today also I invite you to prayer. Only by prayer and fasting can war be stopped. Therefore, my dear little children, pray and by your life give witness that you are mine and that you belong to me, because Satan wishes in these turbulent days to seduce as many souls as possible. Therefore, I invite you to decide for God and He will protect you and show you what you should do and which path to take. I invite all those who have said "YES" to me to renew their consecration to my Son Jesus and to His Heart and to me, so that we can take you more intensely as instruments of peace in this unpeaceful world. Medjugorje is a sign to all of you and a call to pray and live the days of grace that God is giving you. Therefore, dear children, accept the call to prayer with seriousness. I am with you and your suffering is also mine. Thank you for having responded to my call. (April, 1992).

As always, Mary leads us to an ever greater assimilation to Christ. She cooperates with the Holy Spirit in accomplishing this. The Holy Spirit guides us in understanding and living these messages which lead us ever closer to the Heart of Christ:

*. . . I am inviting you, dear children, to pray
for the gifts of the Holy Spirit that you need now,
in order that you may witness my presence here
and in everything I am giving you. Dear children, abandon yourselves to me so that I can
lead you totally. Do not be so preoccupied about
the material things of this world. Thank you for
your response to my call.* (April 17, 1986).

As we live out the messages through our consecration
to the Hearts of Jesus and Mary, we become more closely
united to the Father in the Holy Spirit. We increasingly
conform ourselves in love to God's will—the measure of
growth in the spiritual life. Mary speaks to us about seek-
ing God's will everyday:

*Dear children, today I desire to thank you for
all your sacrifices and for all your prayers. I am
blessing you with my special motherly blessing. I invite you all to decide for God, so that
from day to day you will discover His will in
prayer. I desire, dear children, to call all of you
to a full conversion so that joy will be in your
hearts. I am happy that you are here today in
such great numbers. Thank you for having
responded to my call.* (June 25, 1990).

Isn't she stating that by greater conformity to the divine
will, we are more vitally living out our consecration?
Thus we are surrendering ourselves more to Christ and
to our Mother. We are growing in abandonment to God.
This growth in abandonment is growth in holiness. It is
conversion.

*Dear children! I invite you to decide com-
pletely for God. I beg you, dear children to surrender yourselves completely and you will be*

able to live everything I say to you. It will not be difficult for you to surrender yourselves completely to God. Thank you for your response to my call. (January 2, 1986).

Mary's call at Medjugorje to consecrate ourselves to the Sacred Heart and to her Immaculate Heart provides a profound connection between her teaching at Fatima and at Medjugorje. Just as Mary's teaching at Medjugorje is summarized in the call to consecration to the Hearts of Jesus and Mary, so also is her teaching at Fatima.[24] Also, our mother's teaching at Medjugorje—through her many, many messages—gives a detailed plan of life which allows us to understand all that is involved in living out our consecration. In this sense, Mary's teaching at Medjugorje aids us in living out the message of Fatima— which, again, is centered in consecration to the Heart of Christ and to the Immaculate Heart.

Conclusion

Our Mother's teaching at Medjugorje offers us the way of ongoing conversion—the way of holiness. It is a teaching which, in its own manner, covers the entire path of the spiritual life. It is a plan of spiritual depth, a plan which calls us to happiness and joy:

> *Dear children, today I am blessing you in a special way with my motherly blessing, and I am interceding for you before God that He will give you the gift of conversion of heart. For years I am calling you and exhorting you to a deep spiritual life and simplicity. . .* (December 25, 1989).

> *Dear children, I am inviting you to a complete surrender to God. Pray, little children, that*

Satan may not carry you about like branches in the wind. Be strong in God. I desire that through you the whole world may get to know the God of Joy. By your life bear witness for God's joy. Do not be anxious nor worried. God Himself will help you and show you the way. I desire that you love all men with my love. Only in that way can love reign over the world. Little children, you are mine. I love you and I want you to surrender to me so that I can lead you to God. Never cease praying so that Satan cannot take advantage of you. Pray for the knowledge that you are mine. I bless you with blessings of joy. Thank you for responding to my call. (May 25, 1988).

Dear children: Today I would like to envelop you with my mantle and lead you toward the road to resurrection. Dear children, I beg you to give Our Lord your past and all the evil that has accumulated in your hearts. I want all of you to be happy, and with sin, no one can be happy. That is why, dear children, you must pray and in your prayers you will realize the path to happiness. Happiness will be in your heart and you will be the witness to that which I and my Son want for all of you. I bless you, dear children. Thank you for your response to my call. (February 25, 1987).

Let us not be deaf to Mary's call for she tells how great our role is in God's plan:

Dear children! Today again, I want to call you to begin to live the new life from today onward.

Dear children, I want you to comprehend that God has chosen each one of you in order to use you for the great plan of salvation of mankind. You cannot comprehend how great your role is in God's plan. Therefore, dear children, pray so that through prayer you may comprehend God's plan toward you. I am with you so that you can realize it completely. Thank you for your response to my call. (January 25, 1987).

We should not delay in answering Mary's call or put off our living of the messages. Ivan told us to decide to do better today—we should not wait until tomorrow.

St. Paul tells us that today is the day of salvation: *Behold, now is a very acceptable time; behold, now is the day of salvation.* (*2 Cor.* 6:2). Now is not tomorrow. Now is today, and today is the day of salvation.

nine

The Cross Leads To Life

...and Simeon blessed them and said to Mary his mother, "Behold, this child is destined for the fall and rise of many in Israel, and to be a sign that will be contradicted (and you yourself a sword will pierce) so that the thoughts of many hearts may be revealed." (Lk. 2:35).

Our incorporation into the mystery of Christ at baptism, and our growth in this life, is centered in the pattern of death-resurrection: *Or are you unaware that we who were baptized into Christ Jesus were baptized into his death? We were indeed buried with him through baptism into death, so that, just as Christ was raised from the dead by the glory of the Father, we too might live in newness of life. (Rom. 6:3-4).*

The theme of death-resurrection is at the heart of salvation history. It is a recurrent theme in the Old Testament and in the New Testament.

The Jewish people, under the leadership of Moses, experienced death-resurrection as they were formed into the people of the covenant—Yahweh's people. In the great Exodus event, they escaped Egyptian slavery, went on to Mt. Sinai where the covenant was ratified, and then progressed to the Promised Land. As members of the Mosaic covenant, the Jews experienced a religious transition; they passed over to a higher level of religious existence—to a more intimate union with God.

48

This religious transition contained death-resurrection. For the Jews to become people of the covenant, to remain so, and to grow in the life of the covenant, it was necessary that they undergo a mystical or spiritual death. In short, they had to be willing to pay a price. They had to be willing to bear with that which was difficult in covenant life. This mystical death, however, had a very positive purpose; it was directed at life in the covenant and at growth in that life. This spiritual death, in other words, was for the purpose of resurrection.

Christ perfectly fulfilled the Old Testament theme of death-resurrection. In doing so, He was experiencing a religious transition. He was passing over—gradually, at first, and then definitively in His death—to a new kind of existence, to the life of resurrection. He achieved this life not only for Himself, but for us also. To achieve this new life of resurrection, Jesus was willing to pay the price. He was willing to suffer, even unto death. That it had to be this way—that the only way Jesus could have achieved resurrection was through suffering and death— was pointed out by Jesus Himself to the two disciples on the road to Emmaus: *And he said to them, "Oh, how foolish you are! How slow of heart to believe all that the prophets spoke! Was it not necessary that the Messiah should suffer these things and enter into his glory?"* (*Lk.* 24:25-26).

Christ has structured the Christian life by the way He lived, died, and rose from the dead. It is obvious, then, that the pattern of death-resurrection must be at the heart of the Church's life. Mary, as Mother of the Church and our mother, is in a most advantageous position to show us our own individual roads to Calvary and support us as we carry the cross, each of us on our own as well as the Church as a whole. She already traveled that road in perfect acceptance of the death-resurrection struggle as she was always most closely united with the work of her Son. Individually and collectively, we are meant to continually die in Christ so that we may continually rise in Christ. We thus pass over in a process of continued religious transition to a greater participation in Jesus' resurrection. It is true that our participation in Christ's resurrection will reach its culmination only in eternity. Nevertheless, we begin the life of resurrection here upon this earth, in the here-and-now of human life, in the midst of joy and pain, in the experience of success and failure, in the sweat of our brow, in the enjoyment of God's gifts.

We cannot maintain the life of resurrection or grow in it without a willingness to suffer. This does not mean that we need to feel overwhelmed and heavily burdened by the suffering in our lives. The greater portion of suffering for most of us seems to be an accumulation of ordinary hardships and pains. At times, more penetrating suffering—even suffering of agonizing proportions—can enter our life. Whether the sufferings are either of the more ordinary variety or the rare and extreme type, Christians must convince themselves that to properly relate to the cross is to grow in resurrection.

The great tragedy regarding human suffering is not that there is so much of it, but that apparently so much of it is wasted. Apparently many do not relate to suffering properly—according to God's will. Consequently, they fail to use suffering as a means to growth. Again, our mother's fiat can be a vivid reminder to persevere through even our most difficult trials.

As the opening Scripture passage tells us, Our Lady was no stranger to suffering. As we well know, her life of suffering culminated in her extreme agony beneath the cross. Who can fathom the depth of her grief as she watched her innocent Son suffer the excruciating pain and death of crucifixion? In the church of San Domingo in Puebla, Mexico, there is one of the most striking representations of Mary that I have ever seen. Near the front of the church, and to the right as one faces the altar, there is a figure of our Blessed Mother seated in a chair. She is dressed in a black robe with gold trim. Atop her white veil is a black lace veil of mourning. On her lap is Christ's crown of thorns. Mary gazes down at this crown which had been so cruelly and derisively placed upon Jesus. The expression on Mary's face is one of the most moving I have seen. It is a combination of grief, dignity, and beauty. It is indeed easy to shed tears as one beholds this figure of Mary. It tells us so much about Mary. It tells us that she not only is the Mother of Joy, but also the Mother of Sorrows.

Yes, our dearest Mother Mary knows what it is like to suffer. She knows so well the purpose of suffering in God's plan. By asking her to obtain for us the grace to grow in wisdom, we can increasingly understand the role of suffering in our own lives. Asking her for the grace not to waste suffering, we can learn to use it as a means of growth for ourselves and others.

One of the most traditional forms of the experience of the cross which spiritual masters have always discussed is self-discipline or asceticism. People in all walks of life require self-discipline. The athlete must subject himself or herself to rigorous training; the musician must endure long hours of practice; the doctor must be willing to order his or her life to the vigorous demands of the medical profession.

The Christian life, too, has its own form of discipline, and it is necessary for the greater assimilation of our total being to Christ. Christian self-discipline, or asceticism, helps us grow in the Christ-life. It extends to all aspects of the person—intellect, will, imagination, memory, sight, hearing, taste, touch, and so forth.

Renunciation is another form of dying with Jesus, which, over the years, has been given much attention in the teaching of the spiritual masters. Indeed, the New Testament itself attests to the undeniable role that renunciation plays in the Christian life. The gentle St. Luke, for example, teaches Jesus' message of renunciation—a message which Jesus Himself lived. Renunciation was obviously not the only aspect of Christ's life, but it was an undeniable one. Christians, because they are followers of Christ, must also include renunciation in their lives regardless of their individual vocations. Again, it is well to remind ourselves that we embrace renunciation for the sake of life. This was the purpose of renunciation in Jesus' life, and it must have the same purpose in ours.

Acts of renunciation are life-promoting regarding ourselves and others. Let us always remember what Our Lady of Fatima has said: *Pray, pray, a great deal, and make sacrifices for sinners, for many souls go to Hell because they have no one to make sacrifices and pray for them.*[24] And the angel said to the Fatima visionaries: *Make everything you do a sacrifice, and offer it as an act of reparation for the sins by which God is offended, and as a petition for the conversion of sinners.*[25] All our good actions, including the enjoyable and pleasant ones, can be offered as sacrifices. In the stricter sense, our sacrifices include those actions which involve doing that which is difficult or which involves acts of renunciation.

A good example of an act of renunciation is the practice of fasting which Our Lady of Medjugorje requests of us. She asks us to renounce our regular habits of eating and drinking on Wednesdays and Fridays. Mary tells us that the best way to fast on these days is to partake only of bread and water. If one is unable to fast in this manner, he or she should practice that type of renunciation which is possible. We should remember that fasting is a practice contained in New Testament teaching.

There are, of course, many other forms of carrying the cross besides those of self-discipline and renunciation. There is that very common form of bearing the cross which is involved in the proper living of every day. There is nothing dramatic about this form of suffering, and, precisely because it seems so uneventful, it is difficult to properly relate to it in a consistent fashion. On particular occasions, we might feel that a quick death by martyrdom would be easier than the daily dying which involves all sorts of little sufferings or crosses. But this daily dying is a precious type of suffering, and to grow in the realization of its importance is a significant sign of spiritual progress. It is a sign that we have the spiritual discernment to comprehend that God so often situates the cross within the ordinariness of everyday life.

Crucial decision-making is also a form of the cross. Making a decision, we realize, is extremely important for both ourselves and others. We can seek advice from others, but in the last analysis we know—oh, how well we know—that, ultimately, we alone must make the decision before God. We pray for light and strength, for we realize that we need help not only to make the proper decision, but also to deal with the pain which is inevitably involved.

The experience of failure is another suffering that we encounter in various degrees along the path of life. In failure there is a twofold pain—the pain of having failed and that involved in having to begin again. The pain of having failed must not be wasted. We must use it to become better persons.

Rejection, in various forms, is another pain not uncommon to human experience. Many have experienced rejection because of race or ethnic origin. Although we ourselves might not have experienced this type of rejection, there are other kinds. We may have felt, for instance, a certain ostracism in not being accepted. When our ideas and opinions are not accepted by others, we feel the sting of yet another kind of rejection. And how many there are who have experienced that very painful rejection, being rejected in a romantic relationship.

Another common form of suffering is the experience of loneliness. There are two basic kinds of loneliness— that which need not be and that which cannot be avoided. And who has not experienced the pain connected with illness or injury? Some must bear this cross to a much greater degree than others. Some, indeed, have had their lives very significantly changed because of serious illness or injury. Let us pray for these so that they may have the love and courage to live with their cross according to God's will.

The above examples describe some of the ways in which the cross enters our lives. We can each probably add one or two more to our own list. In any case, we need to remember that we have a special prayer partner to help guide us along the way. She knows suffering and she certainly knows her Son. She is always by our side.

In conclusion, let us again remind ourselves that the cross is meant to lead us to greater life—here and in eternity. Let us always strive to live by the words Jesus has left us: *Then he said to all, "If anyone wishes to come after me, he must deny himself and take up his cross daily and follow me. For whoever wishes to save his life will lose it, but whoever loses his life for my sake will save it. (Lk. 23-24).*

ten

Mother Of Our Christian Virtues

I urge you to consecrate yourselves to my Immaculate Heart, entrusting yourselves to me as little children, so that I may be able to lead you along the road of holiness, in the joyous practice of. . . the virtues: of faith, of hope, of charity, of prudence, of fortitude, of justice, of temperance. . . of humility. (Message of Mary to Fr. Gobbi, #417).

Being mother of our Christ-life, Mary is also mother of our life of Christian virtues. Many of them are listed above, including the three most important ones—faith, hope, and love.

Faith

Ideally, faith is the commitment of one's entire being to the truth of Jesus. We must **live** the truth of Jesus, not merely intellectually assent to it. We properly comprehend religious truth only when we live it, savor it, experience it to the depths of our being. How much more we understand the truth of Christ in its wisdom, power, and beauty when we not only believe this truth with our graced intellects, but also allow it to permeate and transform our entire existence. As a corollary, we see the danger of intellectually assenting to Christ's truth without attempting to live accordingly. Faith can grow weak and even die if there is a constant and serious division between

55

what we believe and the **manner** in which we live.

When we live according to faith, we are living according to a vision of God, humanity, and the rest of creation. Faith tells us things about God and creation we could either not otherwise know or know only with greater difficulty and with less certainty. A good example of the former is the doctrine of the Blessed Trinity. Reason can never arrive at this sublime truth. Only the intellect that has been elevated with the grace of faith can believe in the Triune God. If we are to progress in the spiritual life, we must allow this vision of faith to more and more influence our activities. Increasingly, we should become contemplatives in action. The more we allow Mary to lead us into such a way of life, the more our lives will have meaning for ourselves as well as for the betterment of the lives of people around us. As our mother, she happily guides us to the peace we can find as contemplatives in action.

The vision of faith should inspire us to action according to our vocation, talents, opportunity, time, and energy. We should always strive to make the world more reflective of Christ's image. To the extent we do not, we are betraying the vision of faith.

Mother Mary, deepen our faith. Help us to follow ever more closely the light of faith. And we pray, dear Mother, that you will lead us ever closer to your Son Who is Himself the source of faith's light.

Hope

Christian hope is a virtue that allows us to desire God as the goal of our existence. Hope also allows us to trust that God will grant us the graces necessary to achieve this goal.

The necessity of hope in our lives is obvious. Without

a sustained desire for God we will not be able to live as we should. If God is not our goal, then our lives will be miserably shaped by something infinitely less, whether it be money, sex, social status, or anything else that can grip the human heart as an unauthentic end rather than as a legitimate means to God.

Without God's grace we cannot initially attain supernatural life, we cannot maintain ourselves in it, and we cannot grow in it. At times God allows us to strikingly and intensely experience how helpless we are without Him. Such episodes in the spiritual life can be very painful, but they are also opportunities for great growth. We are meant to emerge from these experiences with an increase of trust in God. We realize how weak we are in ourselves, but how strong we are if we rely on God.

One of Mary's functions as our spiritual mother is to help us grow in trust. In countless ways Mary shows us her maternal love. If we are to love her in return, if we are to allow her to increasingly possess us, we must trust her. In a message to Fr. Gobbi, Mary points out the place of trust for those priests consecrated to her Immaculate Heart. What she says here about trust regarding her priest is proportionately true for all her followers: *Priests consecrated to my Immaculate Heart, my beloved sons whom I am gathering together for the great battle: the first weapon that you must make use of is trust in me. It is your complete abandonment to me.* (#83).

We should always remember: when we trust Mary, we are putting our trust in God; when we abandon ourselves to Mary, we are abandoning ourselves to God.

Love

St. Paul tells us:
If I speak in human and angelic tongues but do not have love, I am a resounding gong or a clashing cymbal.

And if I have the gift of prophecy and comprehend all mysteries and all knowledge; if I have all faith so as to move mountains but do not have love, I am nothing. If I give away everything I own, and if I hand my body over so that I may boast but do not have love, I gain nothing. (*1 Cor.* 13:1-3).

The above words of Paul point out the great importance of the virtue of love. Love is **the** Christian virtue. Jesus Himself has summarized Christianity in terms of love; all the other virtues variously serve love's purpose.

As Jesus walked this earth, His life was a life of love. He mightily loved His Father. With a deep and tender love He loved all members of the human race, and He would die an agonizing and horrible death for them. One of the members of this race He loved in an extraordinarily special way—His Mother Mary. And she was the one person created who could return that love in a perfect way. By following her example, we can also learn to love more perfectly.

The poverty, the hiddenness, the disappointments, the weariness, the joy and the happiness, the pain and the agony—all that constituted the earthly life of Christ was experienced within the framework of love. Jesus loved in everything He did—tenderly, manfully, with understanding and sympathy. He loved with a complete devotedness and a deep, sincere concern for the individual. He loved with a passion for that which is true and good and beautiful. He loved with a complete conformity to His Father's will. He loved always and completely. He loved with a gift of Himself, always pouring Himself out, even to the extreme of death on the wood of a cross. This was the poignant beauty of Christ's life.

Christ shows us His Heart as the symbol of this life of love. It is a symbol which calls for our love in return. The Heart of Christ, source of our own capacity to love, calls us to imitation. Christ, in revealing His Heart to us as symbol of His love, invites us to the closest discipleship as He leads us along the path of love.

We can be tempted to reject this marvelous example of love which Jesus has left us. We can seek our own greatness and fulfillment in a manner which necessarily results in disappointment. We can strive after greatness in ways which God does not intend. These wayward wanderings, however, result in a feeling of dissatisfaction and frustration and we will eventually come to realize they have betrayed us because they are not rooted in Christ and His way of life—the way of true personal greatness.

We grow as Christians as we grow in love. We exercise this love within the milieu of the human condition. This is the only framework we have for achieving our greatness, and, consequently, we must not shirk this human condition. Jesus did not shirk it, but rather accepted it and manifested His greatness within it, despite the pain and even agony that the human condition at times heaped upon Him. It is true that Jesus rejoiced during the course of His life because of the goodness, sincerity, and response of some of those with whom He dealt. For example, the love which Mary and Joseph showered upon Jesus gave Him great joy. During His life, however, Jesus often suffered because of the evil side of humans—their pettiness, cowardice, insensitivity, selfishness, egotism. In other words, Jesus suffered at the hands of others because they were not what they should have been. Nonetheless, these experiences did not thwart the greatness of Jesus. Jesus was always the tremendous lover, and He loved even at those times when it was very painful to do so.

As Christ suffered because of others, we, too, as we try to love, suffer because of others. We may suffer because others do not always understand us—this can be true even of those who dearly love us. We may suffer because some do not appreciate what we do for them, sometimes at great personal cost, or because others reject us, or make us the objects of their meanness and selfishness. We may suffer because there are some who ignore us. At times we suffer so much that we are tempted to quit loving as we should and are tempted to withdraw from the pain of giving ourselves to an egotistic world. To surrender to such a temptation, however, is to forget what true Christian greatness really is—namely, a life of love for God and others, a love that does not shrink from the pain that results from loving in an imperfect world, a love that is meant to become greater regardless of the way others might treat us. Christian love, then, accepts both the pain and the joy of life and carries on under both conditions.

We should ask Mary our mother, who takes such great pride in us when we love as we should, to lead us daily to the Heart of her Son. This Heart, burning furnace of charity, is the source we must draw from if we are to love and progress in love.

Lead us, dear Mother, to this Heart of your Son. As we rest secure in the love of your Immaculate Heart, instill within us daily a growing desire to take on the likeness of the Heart of Jesus. Obtain for us, dearest Mother, the grace to make the Heart of Jesus the center of our existence. Living within this pierced Heart of Jesus, we will more and more be consumed with the desire to love God and neighbor. We will become increasingly aware that to truly live is to love.

Prudence

Prudence is that virtue which helps us to make the proper decisions in the exercise of our Christian life. Prudence aids us in making correct choices so that we do God's will in all areas of Christian existence.

Prudence is meant to influence every aspect of our participation in the mystery of Christ. It is always our guide as we strive to grow in the putting on of Christ. What state of life does God wish me to embrace? What kind of work does he desire of me within that vocation? Among the various ways of expressing love, how am I to love God and others at this particular time? Am I working too much or too little? Am I too dependent upon others or not dependent enough? Prudence helps answer these and other questions concerning the Christ-life.

Some people think that prudence is merely an attitude of caution, an instinct that always leads us to take what seems to be the less dangerous path. True, prudence will lead us to choices of this nature—if God's will indicates this type of action—but prudence is also concerned with the bold and the daring, with taking risks, with magnanimous action. Again, the guiding principle is God's will. The prudent Christian will act boldly or daringly if, after taking the proper means to discern the divine will, she or he decides that God is indeed leading in such a direction.

If we are to be truly prudent persons, we must be persons of prayer. We need the light of prayer to see what decisions are to be made, what actions are to be undertaken. We need the strength of prayer to act upon the given light.

In her earthly journey, Mary was a most prayerful person and a most prudent one. Let us ask our mother to help us grow in the virtue of prudence. The Litany of the Blessed Virgin Mary so bids us to call upon the prudent Virgin: "Virgin most prudent, pray for us."

Fortitude

Christian fortitude, or courage, is that virtue which disposes us to face in mature fashion whatever difficulties we encounter in Christ's service. The necessity of this virtue is evident from our inner experience—we have a tendency to shrink from that which either poses difficulty or frightens us. Apparently, numerous Christians never develop as they should because they do not consistently confront that which is hard and difficult in a proper fashion.

We should not think that courage is a virtue which we need only in times of extraordinary difficulty. As with all the Christian virtues, courage usually finds its expression within the prosaic framework of everydayness. The rather uneventful duties of our state of life day in and day out demands fortitude. All vocations face this challenge, and to evade the challenge is to hinder our growth in Christ.

At times, of course, courage must be exercised concerning matters of great importance, such as the decision involving one's choice of state of life. This type of decision can demand the greatest fortitude in certain instances. Any committed Christian who seriously pursues the development of the spiritual life will, to some extent, experience interior trials of one kind or the other. Whatever form the difficulty may assume, however, the dedicated Christian realizes the need for fortitude.

Mary did not live an easy life. In her greatness of grace, she exercised fortitude on a daily basis. At times she had to draw upon her virtue of courage in a special way. And at that terrible moment beneath the cross, her courage was tested to the utmost. What great sorrow then pierced her Heart! And what extraordinary courage and love it took for Mary to stand by her Son in His most awful moment. Even the greatest pietas of Michaelangelo and others fall short of capturing the awful reality of the scene and the courage it demanded of Mary.

Mary, then, has with courage faced the difficult in extraordinary fashion. In all our difficulties let us fly to the protection of this dear, loving mother. She will help us grow in the realization that facing the difficult is an essential part of being a Christian. She will help us live these words of Jesus: *"If anyone wishes to come after me, he must deny himself and take up his cross daily and follow me."* (*Lk.* 9:23).

Justice

The virtue of justice bids us to give others what is their due. We must respect the rights of others. For example, we must respect the life, good name, and the property of others because they have rights concerning these values. Regarding one's right to life, we have a very timely application of this—the rights of the unborn, and we should all do our part in working against the terrible injustice of abortion. The fatalities which the United States has suffered in all her wars is less than one half of the total number of deaths the unborn suffer in **one** year here in the United States through abortion. And, of course, abortions are being performed all over the world—not just in the United States. In a message to Fr. Gobbi, Mary has said: *Each year, throughout the world, by the tens of millions, innocent children are being slaughtered in their mothers' womb. . .* (#256).

The world of work, professional service, and commerce also involve various applications of justice. The laborer must give an honest day's work and the employer is obligated to pay a just wage. The teacher must realize his or her duty to students by properly preparing classes and professional updating. The doctor must maintain proper medical knowledge in justice to his or her patients and manufacturers of goods as well as wholesale and retail sellers must establish just prices.

The Christian must also be aware of obligations regarding the great social problems that plague one's own country and nations around the world. We must listen to our Mother Mary. She has given us this message: *Come, Lord Jesus, in nations, which have need of becoming once again communities open to the spiritual and material needs of all, especially of the little, the needy, the sick, the poor and the marginalized.* (Fr. Gobbi, #397).

Temperance

The attitude of moderation, which has traditionally been called the virtue of Christian temperance, allows us to relate properly to sense pleasure. God wants us to enjoy what is pleasurable, but He wants us to do so according to His will.

Without an attitude of temperance, a person's life becomes soft and selfish, given over to the wrongful pursuit of pleasure. Insofar as a person's life is thus misdirected, to that extent it fails in service to God and others.

There is an aspect of temperance that one can overlook—that the person who practices temperance enjoys the pleasurable more than does the person who does not. One who lacks temperance is actually a slave to his or her desires. These desires, to the extent they are inordinate, can never be satisfied, and, consequently, become insatiable. Grace does not destroy nature; it brings it to a perfection or fulfillment it could not otherwise attain. Our God-given capacity to enjoy what is pleasurable actually is enhanced by the virtue of temperance.

We should pray, not only for our own growth in temperance, but also especially for those whose very salvation is threatened because of the wrongful pursuit of sense pleasure. Our Lady of Fatima told Jacinta, one of the three young visionaries: *More souls go to Hell because of sins of the flesh than for any other reason.*[26]

Humility

> *My soul proclaims the greatness of*
> *   the Lord;*
> * my spirit rejoices in God my savior.*
> *For he has looked upon his handmaid's*
> *   lowliness;*
> *behold, from now on will all ages*
> *   call me blessed.*
> *The Mighty One has done great things*
> *   for me,*
> *and holy is his name. (Lk. 1:46-50).*

The above passage is a portion of Mary's "Magnificat." One of its lessons is that of humility. In her song of praise Mary expresses perfect humility. She realized that without God she was nothing, but that, because of the divine largess, God had made her great.

Humility is the realization of the truth that I am a creature of God. Humility is also the implementation of this truth in daily living. Humility is not a process of self-depreciation, or of telling myself that I am no good, that I have very little to contribute. Humility moves me to look at myself as I actually am. It moves me to look at both my good and bad points, and, very importantly, to follow up with appropriate attitudes and actions. (Regarding Mary's humility, there was, of course, only the need to recognize her greatness as coming forth from God, since she was completely sinless.)

Since humility is based on truth, it never demands that I deny my particular gifts, my unique talents. Certainly Mary did not do this. If I do not properly recognize my gifts, I will not thank God properly, nor will I be in the most advantageous position for the proper use and development of my talents. I should, then, recognize the good in myself, while simultaneously realizing the source of all good—God Himself.

Humility also enables me to look realistically upon life in the human condition. Being humble means I realize that precisely because I am human, I will experience pain. Precisely because I am exposed to the human condition not only in its pleasant aspects, but also in its dimension of sin, suffering, and anguish, I will suffer—and sometimes because of the wrongdoings of others. Humility allows me to accept this without bitterness, and allows me to react properly.

Humility also assists me in realizing and implementing the truth that I am a social creature—one intended by God to help my neighbor, and, in turn, one intended to be helped by others. It also assists me in accepting my fundamental self. God has created me with certain basic talents, with a certain fundamental temperament. Humility bids me to accept this God-intended self, while always striving to develop, improve, mature.

Humility likewise assists me in accepting my present life situation in so far as I can determine this is God's here-and-now design for me. If I am not properly humble, I can quietly and subtly rebel regarding the present. How unlike Mary, who did not disdain the simple and the ordinary, but rather, found her fulfillment in them as she saw the here-and-now opportunities to say "yes" to God.

We can easily overlook the various applications of humility, so we need to make the special effort to become more aware of humility's role in Christian living. Scripture points out the necessity of doing this:

> *God resists the proud, but gives grace to the humble.* (*Jas.* 4:6).

eleven

Mary And The Church

"Mary is present in the Church as the Mother of Christ, and at the same time as that Mother whom Christ, in the mystery of the Redemption, gave to humanity in the person of the Apostle John. Thus, in her new motherhood in the Spirit, Mary embraces each and every one in the Church, and embraces each and every one through the Church. In this sense Mary, Mother of the Church, is also the Church's model. Indeed, as Paul VI hopes and asks the Church must draw 'from the Virgin Mother of God the most authentic form of perfect imitation of Christ.' " (Pope John Paul II).[27]

In this extremely meaningful passage from his encyclical, *Redemptoris Mater (The Mother of the Redeemer)*, Pope John Paul II tells us that Mary is the Mother of Christ, that she is the Mother of the Church, that she is Mother of each of us in and through the Church, and that she is the Church's model. All of these truths are most intimately connected.

Being Mother of Christ, Mary is also spiritual mother of His members whom Christ has formed into His body, the Church. She is also model of the Church as all good mothers are models for their children. Mary, the best of mothers, is the perfect exemplar, the perfect model, of what it means to be a follower of Christ. She guides the entire Church in greater assimilation to Christ.

If we claim to love Mary, we must also love what she loves. Being Mother of the Church, Mary obviously loves her Church very deeply. As children of Mary, as followers of Christ, we also must deeply love the Church. Sad to say, there are many in today's Church who do not love her as they should. In words to one of her chosen ones, Fr. Don Stefano Gobbi, Mary says:

> *I will bring you to love the Church very much. Today the Church is going through times of great suffering because it is loved less and less by its own children.*
>
> *Many would like to renovate it solely by criticism and by violent attacks on its institutions. Nothing is ever renewed or purified without love!* (Fr. Gobbi, #86).

In loving the Church which is so dear to Christ and to Mary, let us work to further the good which presently exists in the Church, and labor to correct that which should not be. Indeed, there is much good in today's Church. In many members of the Church, there is a deep hunger for a more profound spirituality. There are lay people living exemplary lives, both the married and the single, as they strive to be a light in the market place. There are religious, priests, and bishops who are working with the Holy Father to make the Church more what she should be, in this, one of her most critical hours.

Sorry to say, however, all is not well in the Church. There are deep divisions. Some of the divisions are caused by false teachings. Such teaching has given rise to apostasy and schism.

Mary, however, has launched a counter attack, laboring for the renewal of the Church in many ways. Two of these are: the revitalization of the message of Fatima which is taking place through the Marian Movement of Priests and others; her messages at Medjugorje and the numerous prayer groups and Marian apparitions around the world emanating from the spirit of Medjugorje.

It is up to each of us to do our share in building up the Church, this Church which is the mystical body of Christ. Through our Eucharistic participation, through our prayer and penance—through all our activity done in union with Christ and Mary—let us all strive to bring the Church closer to its model, Mary. Let us work so that the Church more and more reflects Christ as it comes closer to the one who so eminently reflects Christ, Mary herself. In her Immaculate Conception, her fullness of grace, her sinlessness, her bodily assumption into Heaven, Mary indeed is the perfectly and fully redeemed one. She is the one who has been perfectly assimilated to Christ. She is the model the Church more and more strives to imitate. The rest of the Church will never mirror forth Christ as brilliantly as does Mary. We can, however, approach more closely to this ideal who is Mary. Vatican II states:

> "In the most holy Virgin the Church has already reached that perfection whereby she exists without spot or wrinkle. Yet the followers of Christ still strive to increase in holiness by conquering sin. And so they raise their eyes to Mary who shines forth to the whole community of the elect as a model of the virtues. Devotedly meditating on her and contemplating her in the light of the Word made man, the Church with reverence enters more intimately into the supreme mystery of the Incarnation and becomes ever increasingly like her Spouse."[28]

Mary loves her Church with a love whose depths we cannot fully fathom, so we should ask her to help us obtain the grace to increase our own love for the Church. Let us ask her, this dearest and most loving mother, to keep us close at her side as she labors for the renewal of the Church. She invites us to assist her. She tells us:

My cohort is now ready and the time has come. With the weapons of prayer, of the rosary and of your trust, it is now the time to enter into battle.

Soon. . . a new date will be celebrated. The entire Church will flourish under the most pure mantle of your Mother. (Fr. Gobbi, #82).

twelve

The Sacraments, The Mass, And Eucharistic Adoration

"...the liturgy is the summit toward which the activity of the Church is directed; at the same time it is the fountain from which all her power flows." (The Second Vatican Council).[29]

The liturgy is the public worship of the Church. The above statement of Vatican II vividly reminds us that our Christian existence is rooted in the liturgical action of the Church. Two very important dimensions of the Church's liturgy are the sacraments, and—most importantly—the Mass.

Christ offers Himself through the Church and her sacraments so that we might become ever more united with Him. This incorporation into Christ begins at baptism, through which we become a member of Christ and His Church. It means being assimilated to His paschal mystery of death-resurrection, since this was the summary event of Christ's existence. Death-resurrection was the central mystery by which Christ gave us life, and it is the central mystery which each Christian must relive in Christ.

Each one of the sacraments deepens our incorporation into Jesus' death-resurrection. Each one achieves this in a somewhat different manner according to its primary purpose. Finally, and very importantly, each of the sacraments deepens this incorporation within an ecclesial framework. The sacraments, because they are realities of both Christ and His Church, intensify our relationship not only with Jesus, but also with the members of the Church, and with all others also.

Our contact with the death-resurrection of Jesus is most especially renewed and deepened through our participation in the Eucharistic sacrifice—the Mass. It shows the intimate connection between the sacraments and the Mass, as both intensify our assimilation to Jesus in His paschal mystery of death-resurrection.

The Eucharistic sacrifice makes present the Christ-event or mystery of Christ as centered in Jesus' death-resurrection. He, Who was the priest and victim upon Calvary, is also the priest and victim in the Eucharistic sacrifice. Christ becomes really present through the words of consecration. Hence, in an unbloody manner, He makes present the one sacrifice of Calvary. Obviously, we were not active participants in Christ's sacrifice on Calvary. However, in the Mass, Christ invites us to offer along with Him. The Eucharist is Christ's sacrifice, but, by God's gracious design, it is also the Church's sacrifice.

In the Mass we offer ourselves along with Christ Who is chief priest and victim. As Christ's offering of Himself is present in the Eucharistic sacrifice, so likewise is our offering of ourselves. Furthermore, just as Christ's offering on Calvary included everything in His life, so also the offering we make of ourselves at the Eucharist should include all those actions we perform according to God's will in Christ—bearing properly with pain, frustration, failure, misunderstanding, boredom, anguish of spirit—this is what we offer at the altar. Loving another, and being loved by that other, enjoying success, feeling satisfaction in a task well done, enjoying meals shared with

loved ones, drinking in the morning freshness, feeling
the cool spring breeze, relishing the magnificent colors
of autumn leaves—all this we also offer with Jesus. The
Eucharistic offering gathers up what would otherwise be
fragmented pieces of our lives and gives them a marvelous unity, a Christic unity. The Eucharistic sacrifice
unites all these aspects of our lives with the love, the
beauty, and the strength of Jesus' offering and presents
them to the Father in the Holy Spirit with Mary our
Mother at our side. As Mary was present at Calvary's
offering, so is she present as that sacrifice really becomes
present in an unbloody manner in the Mass.

At the Eucharistic meal—at communion time—we
receive Christ in a very special and intimate manner. He
gives Himself to us—body, blood, soul, and divinity.
What an awesome reality! We have to pray for an
increased appreciation of this tremendous Self-giving on
the part of Jesus. We have to pray for the grace to grow
in the determination to love and live Christ more deeply
as we leave each Mass. This ever greater love for Christ,
this ever greater putting on of Christ, should be the result
of each Eucharistic participation.

The Christ Who loves us with an unfathomable love,
Who gives Himself so completely to us in each Eucharistic meal, wants us to allow Him to live in and through
us in an ever greater fashion. If He, in His great love for
us gives Himself completely to us, should not we strive
for our own complete gift of self to Jesus? Obviously, our
gift of self will never equal Christ's perfect gift of Himself
to us, but we can always grow in our gift of self by per-
meating it with an ever greater love. The love of Christ's
Eucharistic Heart, this Heart which for love of us was
pierced with a soldier's lance as He hung in agony upon

the cross, calls for this love of ours. Who can refuse Him? Who wants to refuse Him?

I wish to close this chapter by quoting parts of a message on the Eucharist which Mary has allegedly given to Fr. Gobbi. The message speaks both of the Mass and of Eucharistic adoration outside of Mass:

> *But I am also true Mother of the Eucharist, because Jesus becomes truly present, at the moment of the consecration, through your priestly action. By your human "yes" to the powerful action of the Holy Spirit, which transforms the matter of the bread and the wine into the body and blood of Christ, you make possible for Him this new and real presence of His among you.*
>
> *And He becomes present in order to continue the work of the Incarnation and Redemption and in order to accomplish, in mystery, the Sacrifice of Calvary, which He was able to offer to the Father because of His human nature, assumed with the body which I had given Him. Thus, in the Eucharist, Jesus becomes present with His divinity and with His glorious body, that body given to Him by your heavenly Mother, a true body, born of the Virgin Mary.*

*   *   *

> *With the Church, Triumphant and Suffering, which palpitates around the center of love, which is the eucharistic Jesus, the Church Militant should also be gathered, my beloved sons, religious, and faithful, in order to form, with Heaven and Purgatory, an unceasing hymn of adoration and praise.*

*   *   *

Instead, today, Jesus in the tabernacle is surrounded by much emptiness, much neglect and much ingratitude. These times were foretold by me at Fatima, through the voice of the Angel who appeared to the children to whom he taught this prayer: 'Most Holy Trinity, Father, Son and Holy Spirit, I adore You profoundly and I offer You the most precious body, blood, soul and divinity of Our Lord Jesus Christ, present in all the tabernacles of the world, in reparation for the outrages, sacrileges and indifference with which He Himself is surrounded...'

This prayer was taught for these times of yours.

*   *   *

Jesus is surrounded by an emptiness, which has been brought about especially by you priests who, in your apostolic activity, often go about uselessly and very much on the periphery, going after things which are less important and more secondary and forgetting that the center of your priestly day should be here, before the tabernacle, where Jesus is present and is kept especially for you.

*   *   *

He is also surrounded by the indifference of many of my children, who live as if He were not there and, when they enter church for liturgical functions, are not aware of His divine and real presence in your midst. Often Jesus in the

Eucharist is placed in some isolated corner whereas He should be placed in the center of the church and He should be placed at the center of your ecclesial gatherings, because the church is His temple which has been built first for Him and then for you.

* * *

And so, my beloved ones and children consecrated to my Heart, it is you who must be today a clarion call for the full return of the whole Church Militant to Jesus present in the Eucharist. Because there alone is to be found the spring of living water which will purify its aridity and renew the desert to which it has been reduced; there alone is to be found the secret of life which will open up for her a second Pentecost of grace and of light; there alone is to be found the fount of her renewed holiness: Jesus in the Eucharist!

It is not your pastoral plans and your discussions, it is not the human means on which you put reliance and so much assurance, but it is only Jesus in the Eucharist which will give to the whole Church the strength of a complete renewal, which will lead her to be poor, evangelical, chaste, stripped of all those supports on which she relies, holy, beautiful and without spot or wrinkle, in imitation of your heavenly Mother. (Fr. Gobbi, #330).

thirteen

St. Joseph

. . . the angel of the Lord appeared to Joseph in a dream and said, "Rise, take the child and his mother, flee to Egypt, and stay there until I tell you. Herod is going to search for the child to destroy him." Joseph rose and took the child and his mother by night and departed for Egypt. (Mt. 2:13-14).

Since St. Joseph is the Patron of the Universal Church, it is fitting that we place this chapter on Joseph immediately after our chapters on the Church and the Church's liturgy.

The above Scripture passage reminds us that Joseph was the protector of Jesus and Mary. Being the foster father of Jesus and the husband of Mary, Joseph had the extraordinary privilege and responsibility of taking care of them.

Because of his privileged position regarding Jesus and Mary, Joseph's role in Christianity is both powerful and diverse. Besides being Patron of the Universal Church, he also has many other titles. In the Litany of St. Joseph he is invoked as patron of workers, families, virgins, the sick, and the dying. In papal documents and by popular acclaim he has been hailed as patron of prayer and the interior life, of the poor, of those in authority, fathers, priests and religious, travelers, and because of his closeness to Our Lady, as patron of devotion to Mary.[30]

Let us ask Joseph—this man who enjoyed extraordinary

intimacy with Christ and Our Blessed Mother—to aid us in coming closer to Jesus and Mary. Let us ask Joseph, patron of prayer and the interior life, to help us develop that spirit of silence and prayer which is so necessary if we wish to grow in union with Christ and Mary our Mother.

Joseph will aid us in focusing our attention more and more upon Jesus and Mary. He is a powerful intercessor who desires to help us live out our daily consecration to the Heart of Christ and to the Immaculate Heart of Mary. In Joseph we have a great model in what constitutes this gift of self. Each day he committed himself to Christ and the Blessed Virgin. His gift of self was extraordinary.

St. Teresa of Avila, one of the greatest teachers of the spiritual life, had an outstanding devotion to St. Joseph: "I do not remember ever having asked anything of St. Joseph that he did not grant me, nor can I think without wonder of the graces God has given me through His intercession, nor of the dangers of soul or body from which he has delivered me."[31]

fourteen

Prayer

He went down with them and came to Nazareth, and was obedient to them; and his mother kept all these things in her heart. (Lk. 2:51).

"...and his mother kept all these things in her heart." In other words, Mary prayed over all these things. Mary was a person of deep prayer. How could it be otherwise? The greatness of her grace-life gave Mary an intense and constant desire to communicate with God. Her prayer, focused on Jesus, ascended to the Father in the Holy Spirit.

Mary wants all her children to follow her example. She wants us to be persons of consistent and fervent prayer. How she has insisted on prayer in her various apparitions over the years! Time and time again she has emphasized the necessity and power of prayer. Prayer is essential to our life. It is a dialogue with God.

The Basic Nature of Christian Prayer

Prayer is becoming aware in a special way of our relationship with God and of all that this relationship includes. It is an awareness of God being present to us and we to Him—a presence permeated with love. Prayer is being aware of the all-loving God, and how His love for us is always calling us to a closer union with Him. In prayer, then, we are especially aware of God's love for us and of what our love for Him should be. Sometimes we become keenly aware that God's love is calling us in a very special way. We realize, despite a certain fear of what may be involved, of the necessity to respond. This thought can lead us to another characteristic of prayer—the need to be open before God. Whatever He asks of us, we must give Him; wherever He leads us, we must follow. Our dearest Mother Mary gives us a perfect example. Regarding the Annunciation scene, Scripture tells us: *Mary said, "Behold, I am the handmaid of the Lord. May it be done to me according to your word."* *Then the angel departed from her. (Lk. 1:38).*

Prayer must also be centered in Christ. Again Scripture speaks to us: *In times past, God spoke in partial and various ways to our ancestors through the prophets; in these last days, he spoke to us through a son, whom he made heir of all things and through whom he created the universe...(Heb. 1:1-2).*

Whatever the Father wishes to tell us in prayer, therefore, is in some way contained in Christ. It is our privilege and responsibility to have Christ at the center of our prayer. As we pray with our attention focused on Christ under the transforming influence of the Holy Spirit and Mary, we come ever closer to the Father.

In prayer, the teaching and example of Jesus increasingly penetrate into the depths of our being. The light of prayer shows us that following Christ's teaching and example assimilates us more and more to Jesus. We grow in the desire to come ever closer to His Heart.

The surest way to grow in union with the Heart of Christ is to dwell within the Immaculate Heart. As we pray, then, let us dwell in the Immaculate Heart of Mary and the Heart of Christ. Here we experience love, peace, joy, confidence, and warmth. Yes, Jesus and Mary bid us to pray within Their Hearts. Who can refuse Their invitation?

Prayer Methods

There are various methods of prayer available to us. While not giving an exhaustive list, let us consider some of these. A very fundamental method is simply to talk to God about my life here and now—a life which is a mixture of pain and joy. I can tell Him about my successes, my failures, my frustrations, my joys, my temptations, of that which makes me laugh, of that which makes me cry. In other words, I can discuss anything and everything about my life. I do all of this in a spirit of prayer as I ask God for the light to see how I can serve Him better amid all diverse aspects of my life. I also prayerfully ask for the strength to act according to the enlightenment He graciously grants me.

Another method of prayer involves the direct reading of Scripture—especially the Gospels. I read a verse or two, pause, and prayerfully reflect on how the Holy Spirit desires for me to incorporate this passage into my Christian existence. When I feel satisfied, I read on and pause and reflect as before. I should always remain with a passage as long as I feel I am drawn to do so. At times one passage can serve an entire period of prayer.

Another way to pray is to consider a scene from Christ's life, passion and death, or resurrection. As I present the scene to myself, I observe the persons involved. I consider their words and actions. I ask myself, in the presence of the Lord, how I can incorporate the lessons from this scene of the Christ-event into my own Christian existence.

Another excellent method of prayer which flows very directly from that just mentioned is the rosary. In its own way, the rosary leads us through the Christ event—the life, death, and resurrection of Jesus. Pope Paul VI has stated:

> "As a Gospel prayer, centered in the mystery of the redemptive Incarnation, the Rosary is therefore a prayer with a clearly Christological orientation...The Jesus that each Hail Mary recalls is the same Jesus Whom the succession of the mysteries proposes to us."[32]

Further on, Pope Paul VI points out the importance of contemplation as we pray the rosary:

> "Without this the Rosary is a body without a soul, and its recitation is in danger of becoming a mechanical repetition of formulas...By its nature the recitation of the Rosary calls for a quiet rhythm and a lingering pace, helping the individual to meditate on the mysteries of the Lord's life as seen through the eyes of her who was closest to the Lord. In this way the unfathomable riches of these mysteries are unfolded."[33]

Over the years, in various apparitions, Mary has stressed the importance of the rosary. She has promised great blessings to those who pray the rosary. To St. Dominic and to Blessed Alan she stated:

1. Whoever shall faithfully serve me by the recitation of the Rosary, shall receive signal graces.

2. I promise my special protection and the greatest graces to all those who shall recite the

Rosary.

3. The Rosary shall be a powerful armour against Hell, it will destroy vice, decrease sin, and defeat heresies.

4. It will cause virtue and good works to flourish; it will obtain for souls the abundant mercy of God; it will lift them to the desire of eternal things. Oh, that souls would sanctify themselves by this means.

5. The soul which recommends itself to me by the recitation of the Rosary, shall not perish.

6. Whoever shall recite the Rosary devoutly, applying himself to the consideration of its sacred mysteries shall never be conquered by misfortune. God will not chastise him in His justice, he shall not perish by an unprovided death; if he be just he shall remain in the grace of God, and become worthy of eternal life.

7. Whoever shall have a true devotion for the Rosary shall not die without the sacraments of the Church.

8. Those who are faithful to recite the Rosary shall have during their life and at their death the light of God and the plenitude of His graces; at the moment of death they shall participate in the merits of the saints in paradise.

9. I shall deliver from purgatory those who have been devoted to the Rosary.

10. The faithful children of the Rosary shall merit a high degree of glory in Heaven.

11. You shall obtain all you ask of me by the recitation of the Rosary.

12. All those who propagate the Holy Rosary shall be aided by me in their necessities.

13. I have obtained from my Son that all the

advocates of the Rosary shall have for interces-
sors the entire celestial court during their life
and at the hour of death.[34]

Can we refuse our most loving Mother her request that
we daily pray the rosary? In a message to Fr. Gobbi, Mary
says:

> *Pray with me. All the Church must enter into
> the cenacle of my Immaculate Heart, to invoke,
> with the heavenly Mother, a very special out-
> pouring of the Holy Spirit, which will lead it
> to live the experience of a second and radiant
> Pentecost.*
>
> *Pray above all with the prayer of the holy
> rosary. Let the rosary be, for everyone, the
> powerful weapon to be made use of in these
> times.*
>
> ***The rosary brings you to peace.*** *With this
> prayer, you are able to obtain from the Lord the
> great grace of change of hearts, of the conver-
> sion of souls, and the return of all humanity
> to God, along the road of repentance, of love,
> of divine grace and of holiness.* (Fr. Gobbi,
> #336).

Difficulties in Prayer

What are some of the difficulties, some of the sufferings connected with prayer? To pray well demands a
basic Christian self-discipline that is exercised both during and outside of prayer. If the proper asceticism, the
proper self-discipline, is absent outside of prayer, we can
hardly expect to be properly disciplined during prayer
itself.

Another aspect of the discipline connected with one's

life of prayer is to set a daily time for our formal period of prayer. By formal periods of prayer we mean establishing certain times for prayer during which we put aside all other activities so that we can focus directly and completely on the exercise of prayer. Our Lady of Medjugorje, who stresses so much the need for daily prayer, has told us to establish times for prayer both in the morning and in the evening, as well as allowing the spirit of prayer to accompany us in all we do.

Putting up with distractions during prayer is a difficulty that one often experiences. Only in higher mystical prayer, when contemplative graces are powerfully at work, do all distractions disappear. So we should not expect to completely eliminate these distractions, but to strive to control them as best as possible.

Dryness is another suffering or difficulty we at times experience during prayer. We open ourselves to numerous disappointments if we expect an emotional high to always accompany our prayer. If the emotional high is there we are grateful but if this aspect is lacking we must not be discouraged. Rather, we must realize that the essence of prayer resides in the graced activity of our intellects and wills—an activity which does not need to be accompanied by an emotionally-felt consolation.

Sometimes God just seems so distant. When this happens, we should examine ourselves to see if there is an obvious and significant deficiency in our present lifestyle. Is there something that we are doing and should not be doing, or something that we ought to be doing and are failing to do? If such an examination uncovers no significant deficiency, we can be reassured that this experience of God seeming to be distant is one of the pains or difficulties we can sometimes encounter during prayer's evolving journey. We must also remember, as the lives of Saints tell us, that God can be very close precisely at those times when He appears to be distant. We should try to remain in spiritual peace whatever the difficulty. As the Christian life evolves, it leads to an ever-deepening peace despite sufferings that accompany our growth process. An evolving prayer life, consequently, evolves to a greater peace.

Prayer and Life

Prayer leads us to seek life. During prayer, our relationship with God is deepened. As we open ourselves to God's love, we grow in our desire to give ourselves completely to Him. We desire to hand our complete being over to Christ so that He may lead us ever closer to the Father in the Spirit with Mary our Mother at our side. In prayer we realize that Christ wants to accompany us in all our daily activities. We realize that He wants His teaching and example to increasingly influence everything we do and it gives us the desire to open ourselves more and more to the flames of love coming from the Heart of Jesus.

We need resolve to accomplish God's will each day as we perform our daily duties. Sometimes doing the Father's will is easy, sometimes it is difficult. Whatever the case may be, prayer enlightens and strengthens us for the task.

To live in this manner is a joy, a happiness, a peace. To live in this manner is to make our whole life a prayer. To live in this manner is to live out our consecration to the Heart of Jesus and to the Immaculate Heart of Mary.

fifteen

Queen Of Peace

Tell everyone that God gives graces through the Immaculate Heart of Mary. Tell them to ask graces from her, and that the Heart of Jesus wishes to be venerated together with the Immaculate Heart of Mary. Ask them to plead for peace from the Immaculate Heart of Mary, for the Lord has confided the peace of the world to her. (Our Lady of Fatima to Jacinta.)[35]

The world needs peace. Individual nations need peace and families need peace. The Church needs peace. Each of us individually needs peace. We must work for peace through prayer, fasting, and other Christ-like activities

And just what do we mean by peace? St. Augustine says peace is the tranquility of order. God has put order into His creation and this order must be respected and promoted if peace is to prevail. To the extent that the human family lives according to God's will—lives according to the order or the plan God has established for creation—to that extent does peace exist in the various segments of human society. To the extent there are violations of God's plan, of His will, to that extent peace is absent.

If we are to be instruments of peace, we ourselves must be at peace. Our personal peace is the tranquility of order which results from our doing God's will. The more we are united through love with God in the doing of His will, the more we experience peace.

Sometimes the sense of peace we experience is so strong that we can "feel" it pulsating throughout our being. These are periods of what we may call the experience of extraordinary peace. Unfortunately this type of peace usually is not an everyday occurrence.

Most of the time we live immersed in a more subdued kind of peace which results from our daily attempts to do God's will. It is that peace which is a welcome and sustaining companion as we walk the path of everyday life with its usual assortments of joys and disappointments, successes and failures, laughter and tears.

Occasionally, very deep suffering may enter our lives. It is during these times that we need special determination to preserve ourselves in a basic peace of spirit despite the very significant pain. One may wonder how a person can be at peace amidst the experience of great suffering. St. Francis de Sales in one of his writings—and I have not been able to locate the exact place—offers an analogy which I think is very helpful. He asks us to picture an ocean body of water at the time of a violent storm. The surface of the water becomes extremely turbulent. Francis asks us, using our imaginations, to descend beneath the surface of water into its depths. What do we find? The deeper one descends away from the turbulent surface, the calmer the water becomes. Likewise, says the saint, should it be with us during times of every significant suffering. Although the surface of the spirit may be very agitated, one can still maintain basic peace of spirit by going deep down to one's center where God is more directly experienced. Here the person experiences a calm, a basic peace, although the suffering remains.

If we are trying to do God's will, God intends us to be at peace. The more we conform to God's will, the more we are living according to the order He intends for us.

In turn, the more our lives are in harmony with the order established by God, the more we experience peace— peace being the tranquility of order. The more we ourselves live in this manner, the more fit instruments we become for promoting God's order and consequent peace throughout the various segments of society. Let us ask Mary, to whom God has entrusted the peace of the world, to help us become greater instruments of peace. Queen of peace, pray for us.

sixteen

Adaptation In Christian Existence

. . . the angel of the Lord appeared to Joseph in a dream and said, "Rise, take the child and his mother, flee to Egypt, and stay there until I tell you. Herod is going to search for the child to destroy him!" Joseph rose and took the child and his mother by night and departed for Egypt. He stayed there until the death of Herod, that what the Lord had said through the prophet might be fulfilled, "Out of Egypt I called my son." (Mt. 2:13-15).

As we meditate on this scene from the life of Jesus, Mary, and Joseph, various ideas can come and go. Here are those of a contemporary author, Isaias Powers:

> "Mary and Joseph had placed themselves under obedience to the will of God. The flight into Egypt was part of His will, so they did it. They adapted to new circumstances as best they could. They got on with the job of a new daily routine, living faithfully to God and being true to themselves despite changed surroundings" . . . [36]

All of us must make various adaptations along the path of life. We are members of a Pilgrim Church. Just as the total community which is Church makes adaptations as she progresses through time on way to the promised land—the heavenly Jerusalem—so must each of us adapt to life's changing situations. The changes can be considerable.

The various life stages—childhood, adolescence, young adulthood, middle-age, old age—present us with an ongoing challenge to change. What is appropriate activity for the child is not proper for the adolescent. The young adult must adapt in ways not common to the middle-aged. The changes the elderly must adapt to are not those of previous life stages. To properly meet these various challenges along life's journey is a demanding one. To shrink from the demands of the adaptations involved is to stunt our growth. To make the adaptations, despite the degree of pain, is to develop further that Christ-life of which Mary is the mother.

Personal relationships present us with additional challenges of adaptations. Death takes away a much beloved husband from a devoted wife. Only those who have experienced such a radical loss can fully appreciate the pains of adapting to life without the other. As the wife looks back over the life of the relationship, she will also easily recognize that the relationship with all its joy and suffering, with all its various fluctuations, continually challenged one's capacity to adapt.

Friendship also demands the ability to adapt to the evolving dynamics of a relationship. The partners of the friendship change over the years. Sometimes they both change for the better—and the adaptation required by both is basically a joyful experience. Sometimes one of the friends seems to regress. This puts a strain on the relationship. How should the other re-act?

The adaptation required in today's industrialized-technological culture sometimes seems overwhelming. It is easy to understand, consequently, why Alvin Tofler's book, *Future Shock*, was such a popular publication. He describes the phrase "future shock" as the dizzying sense of disorientation caused by the premature arrival of the future. In other words, the extremely fast-paced change which cuts across various aspects of modern-day life puts a significant strain on one's ability to adapt.

We can similarly consider the spiritual life itself. The spiritual life includes all the various aspects of existence within the human condition. The various challenges to adaptation mentioned above—and the many others not mentioned—are all aspects of our spiritual journey. As the spiritual life develops, we must try to be aware of the dynamics involved. We must try to be cognizant, through good spiritual reading and good spiritual direction of both the general and particularized pattern of spiritual growth.

We say "general pattern" because we all follow the same basic plan in the following of Christ. We say "particularized pattern" because each of us puts on Christ in a way which respects our personal uniqueness. This means there will always be some differences between Christians as they are increasingly assimilated to the one Christ.

Both the general and particularized patterns of following Christ obviously involve change and this change demands that we make adaptations as we progress along our spiritual journey. If we are to grow in the spiritual life, we must follow the lead of the Spirit. This Spirit-led growth will require various kinds of change and adaptation. Sometimes this can be pleasant; at other times, the process can be quite painful. Let us ask Mary and Joseph to assist us in the process, remembering that they, too, had to adapt to changing circumstances—for instance, the changes introduced into their lives by the flight into Egypt.

seventeen

Mary At Cana

On the third day there was a wedding in Cana in Galilee, and the mother of Jesus was there. Jesus and his disciples were also invited to the wedding. When the wine ran short, the mother of Jesus said to him, "They have no wine." [And] Jesus said to her, "Woman, how does your concern affect me? My hour has not yet come." His mother said to the servers, "Do whatever he tells you." Now there were six stone water jars there for Jewish ceremonial washings, each holding twenty to thirty gallons. Jesus told them, "Fill the jars with water." So they filled them to the brim. Then he told them, "Draw some out now and take it to the head-waiter." So they took it. And when the headwaiter tasted the water that had become wine, without knowing where it came from (although the servers who had drawn the water knew), the headwaiter called the bridegroom and said to him, "Everyone serves good wine first, and then when people have drunk freely, an inferior one, but you have kept the good wine until now." Jesus did this as the beginning of his signs in Cana in Galilee and so revealed his glory, and his disciples began to believe in him. (Jn. 2:1-11).

This enigmatic scene gives rise to numerous possible explanations. It is not our intention to play the part of Scripture scholars on this passage. Our goal is to make a few focused remarks as we consider this event in Jesus' and Mary's life.

First, Fr. Raymond Brown, the Scripture scholar, says that Jesus' use of the word woman to address His Mother is unusual. His explanation includes the following:

> In calling His mother "woman," Jesus may well be identifying her with the new Eve who will be the mother of His disciples as the old Eve was the "mother of all the living." She can play her role of intercession, however, only when her offspring on the Cross has crushed the serpent.[37]

It is interesting to note that at Calvary Jesus also refers to His Mother as "woman": *Woman, behold, your son.* (*Jn.* 19:26). The "woman" at Cana and the "woman" at the foot of the cross is indeed the New Eve, our spiritual mother.

On Calvary, Mary, in deep anguish, sees her Son's side pierced with a lance, from which the Church is born. Mary becomes Mother of this Church, Mother of its members. St. Bonaventure, a doctor of the Church, describes this birth of the Church:

> "Then, in order that the Church might be formed out of the side of Christ sleeping on the cross...the divine plan permitted that one of the soldiers should pierce open His sacred side with a lance. While blood mixed with water flowed, the price of our salvation was poured forth, which gushing forth from the sacred fountain of the heart gave power to the sacraments of the Church..."[38]

As Brown points out above, the intercessory power of Mary reaches a definitive stage at the foot of the cross as Jesus gives birth to the Church. However, Mary's act of intercession at Cana should not be taken lightly. It is a foreshadowing of her full intercessory power which would flower later on. The power of her intercession with Jesus at Cana is evident. She does **not** request a miracle. Jesus, nonetheless, using the occasion of her request, performs a miracle as He changes water into wine.

There are those who think that Mary is some sort of obstacle relative to their relationship with Jesus. They falsely think that Mary "gets in the way" as they strive for union with Christ. What a mistaken idea! As Mary's request at Cana brought the attendants into contact with Jesus, so does her intercession on our behalf bring us into contact with Christ. Mary is always eager to bring us closer to Jesus. "Do whatever he tells you," Mary says to the attendants at Cana. She says the same to us. She tells us to follow the teaching and example of Christ, this Christ Who is the way, the truth, and the life.

Mary, as the mother of our Christ-life, is ever eager for us to grow in Christ. As we grow in our consecration to her Immaculate Heart—in entrustment of our total being to her—she helps us grow in our consecration to the Heart of Jesus. Through her maternal activity she aids us in growing in our discipleship, this woman who was Jesus' first and perfect disciple.

St. John Eudes, a great apostle of devotion to the Hearts of Jesus and Mary, says:

> . . ."you are one with Jesus as the body is one
> with the head. You must, then, have one breath
> with him, one soul, one will, one mind, one
> heart. And he must be your breath, heart, love,

life, your all. These great gifts in the follower of Christ originate from Baptism. They are increased and strengthened through Confirmation and by making good use of other graces that are given by God. Through the Holy Eucharist they are brought to perfection."[39]

eighteen

Joy

"Cause of our joy, pray for us." (Litany of the Blessed Virgin).

The modern world, although offering numerous benefits to the human family, has created its own set of evils. One of these is the tendency of industrialized society to put a veneer over many aspects of human life, hiding the beauty which lies beneath.

In the area of human joy, for instance, it happens that we are distracted from some of the very many beautifully deep and simple joys of life by the constant allure of the more superficial, and sometimes dehumanizing, distractions, amusements, and entertainments of industrialized society.

We do not have to think very long to come up with examples. There are many specimens of fine art in our culture, but there is much that is gaudy and cheap. There is also the constant attempt to attract our attention with the sexually alluring. Amid this consistent bombardment of our sense of sight, we can pass over the magnificent works of the supreme Artist. God has touched and adorned His wondrous works of creation with strokes of everlasting beauty. The gorgeous sunset against a blue summer sky, the snow-peaked mountains, the breathtaking colors of trees and flowers and shrubbery adorning the countryside, the fresh and deep greenness of spring, the magnificent reds, yellows, and browns of autumn leaves, the rugged beauty of canyons and gorges—all this is constantly available to us. But are we too distracted with less noble sources of joy?

Do we easily pass over the authentic joy of simple meals taken in the company of loved ones for the false glitter of big, noisy parties where hardly anyone is truly interested in anybody else? Does the joy of seeing the warm, receptive smile of a true friend mean as much to us as striving to strain a bit of joy by buying something we really do not need?

Our culture has a tendency to make us think we have to pay money to really enjoy ourselves. We are led to think that the more money spent, the greater will be our enjoyment. This is ridiculous thinking, of course. Some of the greatest joys in life cannot be bought, as when a tiny tot climbs onto a father's lap and says with a precious smile, "I love you, Daddy." Or when the presence of a loved one makes one feel warm and secure, basking in a quiet glow which reaches deep down where one really lives.

We have to make some effort to enjoy the really real. We have to take time to realize where real joys are to be found, and then have the courage to live by our convictions. Our Christianity, among its many values, reminds us of the very important role joy has to play in human existence. Our Christianity also reminds us to make the necessary effort to distinguish between false and true joy, between the superficial type and the deeper kind. Our Christianity also reminds us that we must make the effort to be joyful always—even during times of suffering. How a type of joy can be present, even as we suffer, we learn from experience. Let us remember what St. Paul tells us:

> *We are treated as deceivers and yet are truthful; as unrecognized and yet acknowledged; as dying and behold we live; as chastised and yet not put to death; as sorrowful yet always rejoicing...(2 Cor.* 6:8-10).

Why not ask Mary our mother to increase our joy? Let us ask her for the grace to grow in the realization that all our various joys, if they are authentic, are connected with our continued growth in Christ. To the extent we live in Christ, to that extent we are truly joyful. Jesus has given these words to a visionary: *"Rejoice in Me and Him Who has sent Me. Do not be...melancholy. BE JOYFUL! Sing praises of joy in Me, and you shall receive My joy. Remember, it is I Who wishes to give you My joy, and for that joy to be complete."*[40]

Yes, Christ is our joy, for He leads us to the Father, in the Spirit, with Mary our Mother at our side. Cause of our joy, pray for us.

nineteen

Ordinariness

He went down with them and came to Nazareth, and was obedient to them...(Lk. 2:51).

These words of Luke conclude his description of the event referred to as the finding of the child Jesus in the temple. They also immediately precede Chapter 3 of Luke's Gospel which begins treatment of Jesus' public life. In between these two events—Jesus' being found in the temple by Mary and Joseph and Jesus' public life—there took place what is called Jesus' hidden life at Nazareth.

During those many years at Nazareth Jesus, Mary, and Joseph lived a very ordinary existence—ordinary regarding the externals of their existence. In fact, so ordinary did their lives appear that one without faith might say that such an existence was rather mundane. Karl Rahner observes: "Let us take a good look at Jesus who had the courage to lead an apparently useless life for thirty years. We should ask Him for the grace to give us to understand what His hidden life means for our religious existence."

Notice, Rahner says *an apparently useless life* (italics mine). In reality, Jesus' life at Nazareth, so ordinary as to appear rather useless to one without faith, was a segment of the greatest human life ever lived. Jesus' life at Nazareth was an aspect of His redemptive effort. What seemed to be such an ordinary life, was, in actuality, an aspect of the drama of Jesus' redemptive work.

We live ordinary lives, too—ordinary regarding their outward appearance. To the extent, however, that we live in union with Jesus and Mary, to the extent that we live with deep faith, hope, and love, to this extent our lives are extraordinary. We truly are living the ordinary, extraordinarily. This is what Jesus wants of us. He says to a visionary:

> Ordinariness is living, laughing, living pure lives, crying, working and growing. It is not chastising, swearing, blaspheming or drunkenness. I do not wish for My people to stop functioning in their daily activities because they have been found by Me! I wish all to carry on lovingly, accepting My many gifts. This is the ordinariness of which I am speaking.[41]

Spectacular opportunities for serving Christ—spectacular in their outward appearance—are relatively few in the span of one's life. We can, however, make each day special for Jesus if we allow Him to lead the way. Then our days are special because Jesus helps us to live them from the depths of our Christian existence. They are lived with great love of God and neighbor and, consequently, are great days in the real meaning of great.

Let us ask Mary, who lived those many years with Jesus and Joseph at Nazareth in a very simple, ordinary style of life, to help us see how the ordinary can truly be extraordinary.

twenty

The Greatness Of The Present Moment

And so I say to you, beloved sons, do not scrutinize the future; and thus neither anxiety nor discouragement will take hold of you! Live only in the present instant, in complete abandonment, close to my Immaculate Heart, the present instant which the love of the heavenly Father puts at your disposal, my little children. . . (Message of Mary to Fr. Gobbi, #81).

These words of Mary, allegedly given to Fr. Gobbi for her priests, can have meaning for all her children.

We can easily develop the habit of belittling the present, not realizing that only the present is completely ours—not the past nor the future. If we wrongfully dwell on the past and the future, we miss numerous opportunities in the here-and-now to exercise our Christ-life. We pass over varied opportunities to be loving, kind, generous, and patient.

Looking ahead to future times, we dream of special opportunities to prove ourselves to be outstandingly Christian, while our neglect of present opportunities is making us terribly mediocre. Or, reflecting upon the past, we squander time mourning missed opportunities while we simultaneously waste the precious chances of the here-and-now.

All this is not to say that there should be no thought of the past or future. Proper recollection of the past, for instance, reminds us of mistakes of those former days and can aid us in avoiding the repetition of such failings. Also, a certain reflection regarding the future is necessary if we are to plan properly. Looking down the path of life as it stretches out before us is also an inspiration to work according to God's will to achieve future goals.

The past and the future, therefore, deserve some of our attention. It is the present, however, which deserves our concentrated focus. Mary our mother again speaks to us. The following words, spoken to her priests, have application to all her children: *The time which the Father still leaves at your disposal is too precious: do not waste it! You should live every moment with me, in my Heart.* (Message to Fr. Gobbi, #90).

Today is the acceptable time. Today is the time of salvation. Today is the time when I can prayerfully meet Jesus, deepen my love for Him, renew my determination to belong entirely to Him. Today is the time when I have numerous opportunities to love my neighbor in quiet but meaningful ways, especially those who are poor, or lonely, or so forgotten in their material and spiritual needs. Today is the time when I can use suffering properly, rather than waste its opportunity for growth. Today is the time when I can be patient and the time when I can be faithful to duty, despite the problems and anxieties. Today is the time when I can rejoice in the Lord, thanking Him for all His wonderful gifts.

Now is the time. Now is the time to live and to love. Now is the time to be Christians according to the Heart of Christ, this Heart which Mary our mother deeply desires us to come to each day of our lives. Now is not yesterday; now is not tomorrow; now is today, and today is the day of salvation: *Behold, now is a very acceptable time; behold, now is the day of salvation.* (*2 Cor.* 6:2).

twenty-one

Involvement With The World

He is the image of the invisible God, the first-
born of all creation.
For in him were created all things in heaven
and on earth, the visible and the invisible,
whether thrones or dominions or principal-
ities or powers; all things were created
through him and for him.
He is before all things, and in him all things
hold together.
He is the head of the body, the church.
He is the beginning, the firstborn from the dead,
that in all things he himself might be
preeminent.
For in him all the fullness was pleased to dwell,
and through him to reconcile all things for
him, making peace by the blood of his cross
(through him), whether those on earth or
those in heaven (1 Col. 1:15-20).

The Christian should have a deeper love for the world
than the nonbeliever. All that is true and good and beautiful, all that we humans reach out for in authentic hope,
all the worthwhile and enthusiastic dreams of the human
heart for a better world, the Christian should be more
concerned about all this than is the nonbeliever. Why?
Because as the above Scripture passage tells us, the world

belongs to Christ. The Christian knows that the human family's pursuit of the true, the good, and the beautiful is ultimately a pursuit of Christ. The Christian knows that any authentic step forward that the human race takes, marks a deepening of the Christic evolutionary process whereby the human family and this world are more closely united to the center and crown of the universe— Christ Himself.

Because the world belongs to Christ, the Christian should feel at home in his or her secular involvement. Obviously, there is a sinful dimension to the world. There are murders, rapes, and blatant sexual promiscuity, and selfish lust for power; there is serious neglect of duty, and a hedonistic pursuit of pleasure. The sinful element of the world, however, should not make us blind to its basic truth, goodness, and beauty.

Obviously, we should not love and embrace the world's sinful dimension. A holy sadness should touch us when we reflect upon the moral depravity that defiles the world's Christic image. We do not refuse involvement with the world, however, because of the world's sinfulness. We often must behave in a way that is different from the way much of the world thinks and acts, yet we must be different in a way that does not make us shirk our responsibility toward the world.

The world in which we contemporary Christians live is a world which is a mixture of that which is true and good and beautiful, and that which is ugly and dreadful and terrifying. We have the privilege and the responsibility of promoting the world's goodness and of lessening its evil influence. We have to aid in directing the human family to increasingly walk along the path that has been made by the footprints of Jesus. This is not always an easy task. There are so many forces in today's world that work against Christ, His message, and the order He came to establish. But are we going to shirk the challenge? Are we going to allow the further pursuit of the true, the good, and the beautiful to be increasingly blocked by the forces of evil?

Mary tells us that the world is headed for a glorious future: *Humanity, renewed by much suffering and by a great purification, will re-consecrate itself completely to the worship and the triumph of God, through the triumph of my Immaculate Heart* (Message to Fr. Gobbi, #60). She also tells us that by our prayers and other good actions we can lessen the chastisement element of this great purification. Mary particularly asks that we pray the rosary to bring about the transformation of the world:

> *Pray with me. All the Church must enter into the cenacle of my Immaculate Heart, to invoke, with the heavenly Mother, a very special out-pouring of the Holy Spirit, which will lead it to live the experience of a second and radiant Pentecost.*
> *Pray above all with the prayer of the holy rosary. Let the rosary be, for everyone, the powerful weapon to be made use of in these times.*
> ***The rosary brings you to peace.*** *With this prayer, you are able to obtain from the Lord the great grace of a change of hearts, of the conversion of souls, and the return of all humanity to God, along the road of repentance, of love, of divine grace and of holiness* (Message to Fr. Gobbi, #336).

Let us pray unceasingly for this transformation of the world in Christ. Besides our prayer, let us also follow the lead of the Holy Spirit in all our other activities so that we may do our share to bring about the glorious new world order of which Mary speaks. We can do this in a spirit of peace and joy despite the various difficulties involved. When we are tempted to become discouraged in the process, let us always turn to Mary. She will comfort us and give us the courage to continue on. How eager she is that we all do our part in leading the world closer to Christ, this world which belongs to Christ, this world which will soon experience a glorious new reign of Jesus Who is King of the universe.

twenty-two

Marian Remarks Of Others

In various places throughout this book, I have quoted others as I have developed the various chapters. In this particular chapter I will offer some further quotations regarding Mary. I will simply allow these Marian thoughts of others to speak to you and me without offering any commentary of my own.

If you will not be submerged by tempests, do not turn your eyes from the splendor of this star. If the storms of temptation arise, if you crash against the rocks of tribulation, look to the star, call upon Mary. If you are tossed about on the waves of pride, of ambition, of slander, of hostility, look to the star, call upon Mary. If wrath or avarice or the enticements of the flesh upset the boat of your mind, look to Mary. If you are disturbed by the immensity of your crimes. . . if you begin to be swallowed up by the abyss of depression and despair, think of Mary! In dangers, in anxieties, in doubt, think of Mary, call upon Mary. Let her name not leave your lips, nor your heart, and that you may receive the help of her prayer, do not cease to follow the example of her conduct. . . If she holds you, you will not fall, if she protects you, you need not fear. (St. Bernard).[42]

Parking in the front of the church, I all but
ran inside and knelt immediately in a back pew.
Words could not express what I felt . . . how great
it was to be back among these people, to hear
the sounds of Medjugorje, to see faces that I
remembered from the first trip and be again
among those so privileged to come here on
pilgrimage. (Wayne Weible, Medjugorje advo-
cate).[43]

Near the Cross of Jesus, Mary stands pointing
to a love intended for the whole world. As the
liturgy proclaims, "He is the Word through
whom you made the universe, The Savior you
sent to redeem us. . . For our sake he opened his
arms on the Cross; he put an end to death and
revealed the Resurrection (Eucharistic Prayer II).
Mary leads each successive generation to
the Cross. There we discover the love of Jesus'
outstretched arms, a love that reaches out east
and west, north and south. (James Cardinal
Hickey).[44]

Mother of grace and mercy, I choose you for
the Mother of my soul. . .O holy Virgin, regard
me as something that belongs to you, and by
your goodness treat me as the subject of your
authority. (St. John Eudes).[45]

In the biblical passages of the Lukan and
Johnanine gospel accounts, Mary is presented as
a woman who is aware of her responsibilities
and conscientious in fulfilling them. She does
not hesitate to take the initiative, where that is
needed. She knows how to be present to every

situation in a discreet and appropriate manner. (Agnes Cunningham, theologian).[46]

Mary is "yes" personified, the personified free acceptance of the divine gift. This is the meaning of her *Fiat* at the Annunciation; she does not choose there what she will do for God but abandons herself freely to everything that the all-powerful Word of God will do in her and through her. (André Feuillet, theologian).[47]

There stood beneath the Cross His Mother, and while the men were fleeing, she stood fearlessly...She looked with pity on the wounds of her Son, through Whom she knew redemption was to come to all. (St. Ambrose).[48]

...the Father willed that she be most highly favored with the gifts of the Holy Spirit. The third Person of the Blessed Trinity, the Sanctifier, filled Mary with His holy presence from the very beginning of her human existence in the womb of St. Anne. She is the masterpiece of the new creation in Christ, the first fruits of his redeeming love. She is the Immaculate Conception. Although conceived by her parents, traditionally Sts. Joachim and Anne, in the ordinary manner, Mary was preserved free from original sin. No other human person in salvation history has ever been so graced by God. (Frederick Jelly, O.P., theologian).[49]

In the Catholic tradition, the mystery of Mary's virginity has been contemplated according to its three principal parts: her virginal con-

ception of Christ...her virginity in parturition
or giving birth to Christ...and her remaining a
virgin after the birth of Christ for the rest of her
life upon earth... (Fr. Jelly).[50]

The full blossoming of Mary's holiness, the
first seeds of which were divinely sown in the
grace of her Immaculate Conception is revealed
in her Assumption into Heaven, where she has
been most joyously and intimately reunited with
her risen Son in glory...What an appropriate
reunion between Mother and Son! Jesus, Who
took His human body from her at the virginal
conception in Nazareth, now in the home of His
heavenly Father welcomes her with the glorified
body that she has received through His resurrection. His redemption of her is complete. (Fr.
Jelly).[51]

...Our Lady told me on June 13th, 1917, that
she would never forsake me, and that her
Immaculate Heart would be my refuge and the
way that would lead me to God. As she spoke
these words, she opened her hands, and from
them streamed a light that penetrated to our
inmost hearts. I think that, on that day, the main
purpose of this light was to infuse within us a
special knowledge and love for the Immaculate
Heart of Mary just as on the other two occasions
it was intended to do, as it seems to me, with
regard to God and the mystery of the most Holy
Trinity.
    From that day onward, our hearts were filled
with a more ardent love for the Immaculate
Heart of Mary. From time to time, Jacinta said

to me: "The Lady said that her Immaculate Heart will be your refuge and the way that will lead you to God. Don't you love that? Her Heart is so good! How I love it!" (Sr. Lucia, Fatima visionary. Jacinta, whom she quotes, was another of the visionaries).[52]

Fr. Kolbe, following in her footsteps, was a man of prayer. He lived the deepest interior life. During the day, many times he invoked Mary and implored her: "Immaculata, tell me how I can draw my brothers and sisters to You!" In jail and in the concentration camp he prayed the rosary and spoke about the divine mysteries with his companions. Even in the starvation bunker where he died he prayed until the last moment: "Ave Maria! Ave Maria!" (Fr. Luigi Faccenda, speaking about St. Maximilian Kolbe, a great devotee of Mary).[53]

We consecrate ourselves to you, holy virgin and mother, because we are consecrated to you. Just as we are not only built up on the cornerstone Jesus Christ, but also on the foundation of the apostles and prophets, so too our life and salvation is ever dependent on...your faith and the fruit of your womb. So when we say that we wish to be consecrated to you, we are only proclaiming our willingness to be, and to accept in mind and heart and action both interior and external, what we really are. By such a consecration we are only making the attempt to carry out in our own life-history the plan of redemption God laid down and in which He has already made His dispositions for us. (Karl Rahner, S.J., theologian).[54]

twenty-three

Lourdes—And My Own Marian Experience

My beloved ones, remain in peace. I am near you at every moment: I am forming you, strengthening you, guiding you, defending you. Guard in your heart the precious pearl of a personal call to live in profound intimacy of life with your heavenly Mother. (Message of Mary to Fr. Gobbi, #346).

In the above message Mary speaks of the personal call which she offers. Since my first pilgrimage to Lourdes marked a very definitive stage in Mary's dealings with me—in her call to me—I am going to utilize this entry on Lourdes to share with you certain aspects of my Marian experience. In none of my previous books have I shared my spiritual experience in such a direct fashion. I am doing so now only because I believe it is Mary's wish that I do so. May my sharing of Mary's maternal love manifested to me be an occasion for your own reflection on Mary's goodness to you.

I have always been blessed with a strong devotion to Mary. I feel this gift is one of God's greatest graces given to me. I remember at an early age often repeating the Hail Mary. Later, I was very much attracted to Our Lady's requests at Fatima. I made the five first Saturdays and practiced what I was told were the other aspects of Mary's Fatima message.

After graduating from college I entered the Jesuits. Our first phase of training consists of two years of novitiate—a period in which one is introduced into the spiritual life according to the Jesuit tradition. This first period of Jesuit training marked a very significant growth in my devotion to Mary.

As I progressed in my Jesuit life over the years, Mary was always a loving, caring mother. I always felt, among other things, that she was a lifeline—always there in a special way at particularly difficult stages of the spiritual journey, not only then, but certainly then. I was not always as loyal a child of Mary as I should have been, but she always kept me aware of her very important role in our lives.

In early 1989 I was in Europe—destination Rome. As I was traveling toward Italy from Northern Europe, I made plans to stop at Lourdes. I considered this a very special stop on my itinerary.

As I left Toulouse on the train for Lourdes, it was raining. Not very far from Toulouse, the rain stopped and the sun appeared. I considered this a gift from Mary:

> *(. . .) How I love you, My son, and what love of predilection I have for you! You must accustom yourself to understand this in so many little things; in so many circumstances which are hardly noticed, such as today, the splendid bright day which I have given you, the blue of the clear skies, the luminous brightness of the snow caressed by the sun, the color of my heavenly mantle under which I ever protect you; the white of my most pure robe with which I wish to cover you* (Message of Mary to Fr. Gobbi, #30).

I walked from the Lourdes train station to the Shrine. It was a day in January, sunny and pleasant, but, as would be expected at that time of the year, there were less than 25 pilgrims at the grotto site. The atmosphere was very special. One realized this was a very holy place. I sat on one of the benches and began to pray. All of a sudden, I was deeply impressed with this thought: "I have finally come home." The thought seemed to come from outside of me, similar to an infused idea. I did not fully understand what this idea meant. I had not seriously strayed from God, so the idea of "coming home" did not mean I was returning as a prodigal son. Nor did the idea mean that I had finally found Mary, since, as I have stated above, I have always been blessed with a strong devotion to her. I was, then, somewhat puzzled at what the words "I have finally come home" meant. My experience, however, was a very profound one as I sat there before the grotto of Mary. I wept tears of peace and consolation. This was to be my first experience of the gift of tears at a Marian shrine. Later I would also experience this gift at Fatima, Guadalupe, and Medjugorje. The gift of tears on these occasions would always be in confirmation of a special interior enlightenment.

In the months that followed, whenever I recalled these words impressed upon me at Lourdes, I was still not sure of their meaning. I did, though, decide to write this book on Mary. I had long wanted to write such a book, but did not feel prepared to do so until now.

In April of 1992 I was given the book, *To the Priests, Our Lady's Beloved Sons.* This is the book which contains the locutions or messages Fr. Don Stefano Gobbi has been receiving from Mary since 1973. This book has made a profound impression on me.

Soon after I began to read this particular book, Mary revealed her will for me—which, of course, is God's will for me—in an extraordinary fashion. This special manifestation, the reading of the above-mentioned book, and other recent events, have had a profound impact upon me and have very significantly deepened my spiritual life. This deepening continued in a very special way through my recent pilgrimages to Fatima, Lourdes, Guadalupe, and Medjugorje.

I was privileged to be at Fatima for the 75th anniversary of the October 13 apparition of Mary to the three young visionaries—Lucia, Jacinta, and Francisco. I had a conviction that Mary wanted me there at that particular time. That I was able to be present for this momentous occasion was another special gift of Mary to me.

On October 12, the eve of the anniversary day, I was praying in the basilica at Fatima. I was close to the altar. In the sanctuary was a statue of Our Lady of Fatima. I prayed that Mary would draw me closer than ever to the Heart of Jesus and to her own Immaculate Heart. I also prayed that I would be able, as never before, to work for the spread of devotion to the Hearts of Jesus and Mary.

As I prayed I would often glance at Mary's statue, and when I did, I was often given the gift of tears—I know it was a special gift because I myself had no control over when this would or would not take place. The same thing happened the next day. It was a most profound spiritual experience—even more so than the one at Lourdes.

On the 13th itself, there were about one million pilgrims present for the anniversary occasion. At communion time of the outdoor Mass I felt a special confirmation of the above-mentioned experience.

From Fatima I went to Lourdes. This time, unlike my first visit, I was present along with thousands of other pilgrims. It is indeed a special experience to be at Lourdes with so many others for the impressive candlelight rosary procession at night and for other activities. Being personally present amidst all this gives one a sense of why Lourdes has been such an attraction for millions and millions of pilgrims over the years. Again, my experience at the grotto of Our Lady was very special, as was the making of the Way of the Cross on the hill high above the basilicas and the grotto.

A few months after my visits to Fatima and Lourdes I was at the Shrine of Our Lady of Guadalupe in Mexico City. It was another special gift to be able to be there for the Feast of Our Lady of Guadalupe on December 12. What an inspiration it is to be there on this most special day—to see the Mexican people come from miles and miles away for this feast which is so dear to their hearts. Their devotion to Our Lady is most remarkable. Regarding myself, the entire pilgrimage prior to the feast day was rather subdued—peaceful, but no special experience. I remained in such a state on the feast itself up to and including most of the Mass at the Shrine. Then at communion time I was gifted with the same type of deep experience which had occurred at Lourdes and Fatima. I was rather suddenly struck with a deep conviction that I am protected by Mary's mantle and that I should not be afraid or worry. Again, this interior enlightenment was accompanied by the gift of tears.

My final pilgrimage was to Medugorje—December 28, 1992, to January 4, 1993. Again, after prayer, I had developed the conviction that Mary wanted me there for her great feast of January 1st—which, of course, is the feast of Mary, Mother of God. I thought something special would happen on that day, although I did not know precisely what.

As was the case at Guadalupe, nothing out of the ordinary happened to me on the days previous to January 1. I did not see any phenomena concerning the sun which many pilgrims have observed over the years at Med-jugorje. The chain on my rosary did not change to gold—as has occurred with many of the Medjugorje pilgrims. But Mary did have her gift for me. Just as I had hoped, something special did occur on the feast of January 1. At Mass, after receiving communion, I received a profound experience of Mary's motherhood toward me and also a profound conviction of Jesus' love for me. This conviction of Jesus' love for me may be the most special I have ever experienced. Again, these interior enlightenments were accompanied by the gift of tears.

Later that day I had the great privilege of being present in the choir loft for the daily apparition of Our Lady. Ivan was the only visionary present in Church this particular day. Although I felt extremely blessed to be present for the apparition—which, of course, only Ivan himself could see—I had no special inner experience at this time. Others in our group said they did have a special personal experience at the time of the apparition. My special experience of the day had indeed occurred earlier at Mass.

Since that first visit to Lourdes when I was suddenly struck with the thought, "I have finally come home," much has happened regarding my relationship with Mary. I now believe I know the meaning of those words impressed upon me at Lourdes in January, 1989. More than three years later Mary began to instruct me regarding the precise meaning of those words. She has, in her maternal love for me, entered my life as never before. She has led me to consecrate myself to the Heart of Christ and to her Immaculate Heart in a very meaningful manner. In an extraordinary fashion she has given me a mission to fulfill in the service of Jesus. As she cooperates with the Holy Spirit in my ongoing transformation in Christ, she is leading me along paths which I have never traveled before. I can never thank her adequately for her goodness to me.

The above constitutes some of the main aspects of my personal Marian pilgrimage over the years. You also have your own Marian experience, and I am sure you have shed your own tears of joy and peace along the way.

If you have not yet done so, I strongly encourage you to consecrate yourself to the Heart of Jesus and to the Immaculate Heart of Mary. In consecrating yourself to Mary—in entrusting yourself entirely to her—you will be enabling her to lead you ever closer to the Heart of Christ. She will accomplish marvels in you as she aids you, in cooperation with the Holy Spirit, in living out your consecration to the Sacred Heart. Indeed, she will ever be Mother at your side as you come closer to the Father through Christ and in the Holy Spirit.

I have never been happier, never more at peace, than I presently am. Since Mary has drawn me to consecrate myself to her Immaculate Heart, marvelous changes have taken place within me. She has brought me to the Heart of Jesus in a way I had not experienced before.

If you have given yourself totally to Mary—and this is what consecration to her Immaculate Heart means—you have had similar experiences.

Having consecrated ourselves to Mary, we feel secure as we rest in her loving, maternal Heart. There she comforts us when we are sad—there she wipes away our tears. There she rejoices with us when we rejoice. There she smiles as we share with her our accomplishments for Christ. There she encourages us when we are fearful. There she strengthens us for the most difficult tasks.

What a great gift Jesus has bestowed upon us in giving Mary to us as our mother! Let us thank Him each day for this Mother who loves us with an unfathomable love. We must try to grow in the appreciation of this love. The more we do so, the more we want to cry out, "O Mother, how loving, caring, and tender you are! Draw us ever closer to your Immaculate Heart where you accomplish your marvels within us."

twenty-four

Mother At Our Side—
Concluding Remarks

Why do you doubt? Why are you sad? I am at your side at all times; I never leave you. I am a mother and I am drawn close to you by the weight of the great difficulties in which you are living today. (Message of Mary to Fr. Gobbi, #327).

These words which Mary has given to Fr. Gobbi for her priest-sons remind us that Mary is at the side of all her children—loving them, desiring to protect them.

Yes, Mary is mother at our side inviting us to consecrate ourselves to her Immaculate Heart so that she may assist us in living out our consecration to the Heart of Christ. All that we have said in this book has a relationship to our consecration to the Hearts of Jesus and Mary.

Remember that in this consecration we give ourselves, we entrust ourselves, entirely to Jesus and Mary. This consecration summarizes the spiritual life: through and with Jesus we go to the Father in the Holy Spirit, with Mary our mother at our side.

Currently Mary is telling us in many ways that our act of consecration, and the daily living of that consecration, is critically important. We live in extremely critical times, and Mary is asking for our help regarding the renewal of the Church and the entire world.

122

She tells us that the Church and all humanity is headed for a glorious new era—but that a great purification is required before this will occur. She tells us that we are already experiencing a portion of this purification, and that it will become more intense in order to prepare the Church and the world for a period of profound peace and splendor. Mary calls for our lives of holiness to help bring about this wondrous state of existence, a state in which Jesus will reign in a most glorious fashion. Our lives of consecration—our lives of holiness—as they contribute to the purification process, lessen the chastisement element of the procedure.

It is a great blessing to be alive at such a momentous period of the Church's and world's existence. As we answer Mary's call, she desires us to do so in a spirit of peace and joy. She does not hide the rigors of the purification which Church and world might endure. She does, however, tell us to cast aside morbid fear and to trust in the Lord. God never asks us to endure anything without giving us the proportionate grace to accomplish His will. God desires that we always strive to fulfill His will in a spirit of peace, joy, and happiness.

Mary has been given to us as light to guide us safely through the momentous and critical times in which we live. In a message to her priests, Mary says:

> *My beloved sons, the more this darkness will descend upon the world and into the Church, the clearer will be the light which will shine forth from my Immaculate Heart to show you the way.*
> *Walk in this light. Thus you will always be filled with light.* (Message to Fr. Gobbi, #116).

Mary, Our Lady of Light, leads us to Christ Who is Light of the world:

> *Do not become disturbed by the darkness which has spread about, because this is part of the plan of my Adversary; it is on the other hand part of my own victorious plan, namely, that of dispelling the darkness so that the light may everywhere return.*

> *And the light will shine resplendently throughout creation when it will once again sing the love and glory of God, following on the defeat of every form of atheism and of proud rebellion.*
> *The light of truth, of fidelity and of unity will once again shine fully in the Church. My Son Jesus will manifest Himself fully in such a way that the Church will become light for all the nations of the earth.*
> *I will make the light of grace shine in souls. The Holy Spirit will communicate Himself to them in superabundance, in order to lead them to the perfection of love...*(Message to Fr. Gobbi, #200).

And, again:

> *Today you recall with joy the sign which, sixty years ago, I gave in this place chosen by me to manifest myself. You call it the miracle of the sun.*

> *Some of those present in this place today are thinking: 'What a great marvel it would be if the miracle of the sun were to be repeated!'*

But every day I repeat it for each one of you: when I lead you along the pathway of My Son; when I help you to be healed of sin; when I lead you to prayer, and when I form you to holiness, it is the light of this sun that I cause to shine ever more brightly in your souls and your lives: the sun of my Son Jesus.

And so the miracle of the sun which took place here was but a sign. The eyes of those present perceived this extraordinary phenomenon which caused many to believe in the action of your Mother whose duty it is to set burning in the hearts of all men the light of Jesus, the true Sun of the World. (Message of Mary given to Fr. Gobbi at Fatima, October 13, 1977, the Sixtieth Anniversary of the Last Apparition. Message #137).

Let us close out our thoughts on Mary, *Mother at Our Side,* by reflecting upon some of the words which Our Lady of Guadalupe has given to us through her servant Juan Diego. I think these words are among the most beautiful and consoling which Mary our Mother has given to us her children. A portion of these words are inscribed above the main entrance of the Basilica Church at the Shrine of Our Lady of Guadalupe:

Know for certain that I am the perfect and perpetual Virgin Mary, Mother of the True God. . .here I will show and offer all my love, my compassion, my help and protection to the people. I am your merciful Mother, the Mother of all who love me, of those who cry to me, of those who have confidence in me. Here I will hear their weeping and their sorrows. . .their necessities and misfortunes. . . Do not be troubled or weighed down with grief. Do not fear any illness or vexation, anxiety or pain. Am I not here who am your Mother? Are you not under my shadow and protection? Am I not your fountain of Life? Are you not in the folds of my mantle? In the crossing of my arms? Is there anything else you need?[55]

Notes

1. *The Documents of Vatican II* (New York: The America Press, 1966), *Dogmatic Constitution on the Church,* No. 61.
2. Ibid., No. 62.
3. Ibid., No. 60.
4. Pope John Paul II, *The Mother of the Redeemer (Redemptoris Mater)* (Washington: United States Catholic Conference, 1987), No. 38.
5. Ibid., No. 45.
6. Ibid., No. 45.
7. John Cardinal Newman, *Discourses Addressed to Mixed Congregations* (London: Longmans, Green and Co., 1906), pp. 111-12.
8. A. Bossard, in *Dictionary of Mary* (New York: Catholic Book Publishing Co., 1985), p. 55.
9. Pope Pius XII, *Haurietis Aquas* (New York: Paulist Press), No. 139.
10. Archbishop R. Arulappa, *The Two Hearts,* in *The Fatima Crusader,* Summer, 1992, p. 3.
11. *To the Priests, Our Lady's Beloved Sons,* published by The Marian Movement of Priests, St. Francis, Maine. Hereafter, whenever I quote from this book, I will merely give the chapter number beside the quoted passage in the body of the text. This book, which contains Mary's messages or locutions to Fr. Don Stefano Gobbi, may be obtained free of charge, although voluntary contributions allow its free distribution. In the U.S.A. English, French, Spanish, and Italian copies may be obtained by writing to:
The Marian Movement of Priests
P.O. Box 8
St. Francis, Maine 04774-0008

In Canada, copies (English only) may be obtained by writing to:
The Marian Movement of Priests
1515 Bathurst Street
Toronto, Ontario M5P 3H4

12. Pope John Paul II as quoted by Fr. Paul Leonard in *The Fatima Crusader,* Summer, 1992, p. 18.
13. *Our Lady's Peace Plan from Heaven,* (Rockford: TAN Books and Publishers, Inc., 1983), p. 14.
14. Ibid., p. 30.
15. Ibid., p. 31.
16. Ibid., p. 23.
17. St. Louis de Montfort, *God Alone: The Collected Writings of St. Louis de Montfort* (Bay Shore: Montfort Publications, 1987), p. 266.
18. Karl Rahner, *Spiritual Exercises* (New York: Herder and Herder, 1965), pp. 244-47.
19. *Our Lady's Peace Plan,* op. cit., p. 10.
20. Ibid., p. 3.
21. *I Am Your Jesus of Mercy* (Milford: The Riehle Foundation, 1989), Vol. I, pp. 39-40.
22. The Medjugorje messages are taken from D. R. Golob, *Live the Messages,* and, regarding those after February, 1991, from The Marian newspaper, *A Call to Peace,* published at Bella Vista, Arkansas. *Live the Messages* may be obtained—among other places—from The Riehle Foundation, P.O. Box 7, Milford, Ohio 45150).
23. I am indebted to more than one source for historical facts concerning Medjugorje. I would particularly like to acknowledge Mary Joan Wallace's book, *Medjugorje: Its Background and Messages* (Huntington Beach: Follow Me Communications, Inc., 1991).
24. *Our Lady's Peace Plan,* op. cit., back cover.
25. Ibid., p. 1.
26. Ibid., p. 9.
27. *The Mother of the Redeemer,* op. cit., No. 47.
28. Vatican II, *Constitution on the Church,* op. cit., No. 65.
29. Vatican II, *Constitution on the Liturgy,* No. 10.
30. *New Catholic Encyclopedia* (New York: McGraw Hill Book Company, 1967), Vol. VII, p. 1111.
31. Michael Gasnier, O.P., *Joseph the Silent* (New York:

Kennedy & Sons, 1962), p. 9.

32. Pope Paul VI, *Devotion to the Blessed Virgin Mary* (*Marialis Cultus*) (Washington: United States Catholic Conference, 1974), No. 46.

33. Ibid., No. 47.

34. *The Fatima Crusader,* Summer, 1992, p. 30.

35. *Our Lady's Peace Plan,* op. cit., p. 10.

36. Isaias Powers, *Quiet Places with Mary,* (Mystic: Twenty-Third Publications, 1986), p. 38.

37. Raymond Brown, S.S., *The Gospel of St. John* and *The Johannine Epistles* in *New Testament Reading Guide* (Collegeville: Liturgical Press, 1960), Vol. 13, p. 23.

38. *Bonaventure,* translated by Evert Cousins (New York: Paulist Press, 1978), pp. 154-55.

39. St. John Eudes, in *The Liturgy of the Hours* (New York: Catholic Book Publishing Co., 1975), Vol. IV, p. 1332.

40. *I Am Your Jesus of Mercy,* op. cit., Vol. III, p. 7.

41. Ibid., Vol. II, p. 44.

42. St. Bernard, in Hilda Graef, *Mary: A History of Doctrine and Devotion* (Westminster: Christian Classics and London: Sheed & Ward, 1985), Vol. I, p. 237.

43. Wayne Weible, *Medjugorje: The Message* (Orleans: Paraclete Press, 1989), p. 156.

44. James Cardinal Hickey, *Mary at the Foot of the Cross* (San Francisco: Ignatius Press, 1988), p. 127.

45. St. John Eudes, in *Mary: A History of Doctrine and Devotion,* op. cit., Vol. II, p. 41.

46. Agnes Cunningham, *The Significance of Mary* (Chicago: Thomas More Press, 1988), p. 28.

47. André Feuillet, *Jesus and His Mother* (Still River: St. Bede's Publications, 1984), p. 205.

48. St. Ambrose, in *Mary: A History of Doctrine and Devotion,* op. cit., Vol. I, p. 82.

49. Frederick Jelly, O.P., *Madonna: Mary in Catholic Tradition* (Huntington: Our Sunday Visitor Publishing Division, 1986), p. 100.

50. Ibid., p. 78.

51. Ibid., p. 117.

52. Louis Kondar, SVD, editor, *Fatima in Lucia's Own Words* (Fatima: Postulation Centre, 1976), p. 111-12. Distributed

in the U.S.A. by the Ravengate Press, Cambridge, MA.

53. Luigi Faccenda, O.F.M. Conv., *One More Gift* (West Covena: Immaculata Press, 1990), p. 68.

54. Karl Rahner, S.J. *Mary, Mother of the Lord* (Wheathampstead: Anthony Clarke Books, 1963), p. 106.

55. Francis Johnson, *The Wonders of Guadalupe* (Rockford: TAN Books & Publishers, Inc., 1981), inside cover.

Faith Publishing Company

Faith Publishing Company has been organized as a service for the publishing and distribution of materials that reflect Christian values, and in particular the teachings of the Catholic Church.

It is dedicated to publication of only those materials that reflect such values.

Faith Publishing Company also publishes books for The Riehle Foundation. The Foundation is a non-profit, tax-exempt producer and distributor of Catholic books and materials worldwide, and also supplies hospital and prison ministries, churches and mission organizations.

For more information on the publications of Faith Publishing Company, contact:

Faith Publishing Company
P.O. BOX 237
MILFORD, OHIO 45150